AN ANDREW GREELEY READER

Volume I

Edited by John Sprague

Thomas More Press
Chicago, Illinois

ISBN 0-88347-215-5

Contents

Introduction

SIXTEEN years ago, Catholic book publishing was in such a depressed state that the Thomas More Book Club was experiencing difficulty finding enough good books to offer its members. There seemed to be only one solution to the problem: we would have to begin publishing books ourselves. Our first venture would be a series of original paperbacks under the title *What a Modern Catholic Believes*. . . . It was vitally important that our leadoff book not only reflect the latest in theological thought, but that it be creative, lively and, most of all, readable. Our choice of author was easy. Andrew Greeley wrote *What a Modern Catholic Believes about God*, the series was a great success, and Thomas More Press was quickly and firmly established.

Since that time, Father Greeley has authored or coauthored twenty other books for Thomas More Press, analyzing Catholic teachings and practices (often with the assistance of sociological data), postulating explanations for the widespread dissatisfaction during these changing times, and proposing solutions and "new agendas." This list of books is a testament not only to his creativity and rightness of thinking, but to his prophetic sense as well. And it is especially noteworthy that so many of Father Greeley's ideas, analyses and proposals have survived the tests of time and trends. Many of these books are no longer available simply because the economics of publishing dictate that, after a certain point, further printings are not financially wise—even not-for-profit publishers have to at least break even. Declaring a book out-of-print is an especially onerous task when you know that it is still just as topical as the day it was written. Such was the case with several of Father

Greeley's books, and each time we had to cross one off our list it was not without a sense of loss and more than a twinge of guilt.

But, as we all know, guilt is cumulative, and it became obvious to us that the mounting weight of the Andrew Greeley out-of-print list demanded some form of atonement. We decided to look over all of these books with the intention of finding one or more that might be an obvious candidate for republication. However, in rereading them we found there were too many obvious choices. So we realized that it would be an even better idea to collect passages from them (in effect resurrecting them all, albeit in a greatly abridged form) that would give us a representative survey of this extremely impressive body of work.

The chapter headings for the *Andrew Greeley Reader,* therefore, represent topics that Father Greeley has addressed at length using his experience and skills as priest, theologian, and social analyst. They correspond with some of the major elements of concern to the church over the past twenty years, such as: defining church, the priesthood, women in the church, sexual teaching and sexuality, and the "new agenda"—where we go from here. And they are topics that are constantly being redefined.

The excerpts I have gathered for this volume obviously do not present a complete overview of Father Greeley's works (hence the designation volume one) since they have been extracted from Thomas More Press publications. But they do indicate the enormous contribution he has made to the church in America over the past twenty-plus years.

John Sprague

Chapter One

———

What a Modern Catholic Believes About the Church

A TALE OF TWO PARISHES

THE juridic-structural approach to the Church has been so much a part of our cognitive training that it is very difficult for us to put it aside temporarily and approach the Church from the other end; that is to say, the "end" of the grassroots community. If I am to be successful in leading the reader to begin to think about the Church from this perspective—a perspective which I argue is fundamentally much more important to him—I must first of all touch a responsive chord somewhere in his personality. I must find a way to release in him the complex assemblage of positive and negative feelings that he has experienced in the past about the local community that is his Church. When the reader and I are able to share some of the vivid emotions that we have experienced in our local communities, then we may be able to examine these emotions, and the reality which has occasioned such emotions.

I therefore propose to begin by describing the two parish communities that have meant the most to me in my own life—St. Ursula parish where I grew up and St. Praxides parish where I served for the first decade of my life in the priesthood. I cannot expect that the reader will have lived in parishes exactly like St. Ursula and St. Praxides, but if I am skillful enough in describing these two experiences which were so fantastically important to me, then the reader may begin to recall his own experiences of local communities. Then, we can talk about the Church.

St. Ursula was a Depression parish. Its streets were lined by tidy 1920 bungalows and two-flats. Its Irish parishioners (along with a handful of Italians) were solid, respectable members of the lower-middle class (spiced up by a few professionals and business executives like my father) but it was a time of economic stagnation and limited expectations. A job in hand was worth more than a college education. WPA had paved our streets but by the late

1930s most of the members of the parish were employed. They were not, however, so secure in their jobs that the purchase of a new radio was not a major expenditure. It was a parish of street-cars and buses. Many of us did not have cars and even those who did were disinclined to let their teenage children drive them. One went to school, to the show, the pool halls and the drugstores on foot, and if one was old enough to court, one frequently courted on long walks and on bus rides. It was a parish with a frame church which was eventually replaced by a gymnasium that served as a "temporary church" for almost two decades. It was a parish of street corners, of baseball in "prairies," and of touch football on the asphalt alongside our corner house. It was a parish of snowball fights with the "publics" during the wintertime and of basketball in back of garages in the summer. It was a parish of a kindly, gray-haired monsignor in failing health and of affable, wise-cracking curates (and of one curate who had us reciting the dialogue Mass and belonging to organized Catholic action groups in the middle of the 1930s). It was a parish of nuns (all but one of our school teachers were nuns), some of whom were "nice" and others of whom were "crabs"—in about equal proportions as I remember. It was a parish of oppressive, dull religion books and of fascinating history and geography books, of "Palmer Method" prizes (though I never won one) and of Superiors who carried little hand bells that they compulsively sounded whenever faced with a crisis. It was a parish of carnivals and raffles, of novenas and missions (usually featuring incredibly bad sermons), of orderly "ranks" coming out of the parochial school, of crowded Sunday Masses with collection envelopes and sparse weekday Masses invariably said in black vestments. It was a parish where some of our more venturous teenagers enjoyed breaking up the camp meetings of our Protestant brothers (not brothers then) held in the summer-time and of suspicious Greek ice-cream parlors where we were attracted by the vast scoops of whipped cream and frightened by the dark, swarthy males with (heaven forbid) long sideburns. (What

12

we thought about the lovely Greek waitresses at these ice-cream parlors probably ought not to be here recorded.) It was a parish in which some of us, at least, looked up the Legion of Decency listing on a movie before we went to the "Manor" or the "Iris" and a parish where repeated attempts at collection drives to build our "new church" were greeted with complaint, dismay, and enthusiasm, though, in Depression years, rarely with success.

St. Ursula was a stable community, closed, loyal, warm—for many of us, the center of our lives. We were not then people of plenty; it was not an age of affluence. We were not inclined, most of us, to look beyond the religious or socioeconomic or eductional borders of our parish. It was a gray-tinted world where we did not expect much and where both our anticipations and our disappointments were carefully controlled by the great and somber pall of the Depression.

Yet, for many of us the parish was the center of our lives (though we would hardly have thought of it, much less described it, in those terms). If we were asked where we were from we would not say Austin or Mayfield Avenue; we would say St. Ursula. So much of our "identity" (though we wouldn't have known the word then) was Irish Catholic that our geography was expressed in Irish Catholic terminology. It is important to emphasize, however, that we were not Irish Catholic consciously or explicitly; it was something we assumed, something that was almost as pervasively a part of our lives as the air we breathed.

Later I would come to understand the dynamics that went into the construction of St. Ursula and I would know that it was an "immigrant parish," though I am sure we would not have thought of it as such in those days and the implication that we were "immigrants" and thus something less than fully American would have been offensive indeed.

I am gentle in my description of St. Ursula, perhaps even nostalgic, though I liked it even in the 1930s and was proud of it. Those of us who went off from it to the seminary were determined to sing its praises despite the taunts about our basement church. There were immigrant parishes of the 1930s that gave one much less to be proud of than did St. Ursula, and yet the criticism that one hears from Catholic liberal intellectuals about the parish in which they grew up frequently misses the point. The St. Ursulas of the country were, indeed, narrow and, in the fullest sense of the word, parochial. It's hard to see, given the social and economic condition of the Catholic population of that time, how they could have been much else. It's easy to be a social critic from the perspective of hindsight. If one evaluates St. Ursula from the perspective of the 1970s it appears very inadequate. Its theology was unsophisticated to the point of being simplistic. Its liturgy was generally meaningless ritual. Its worldview did not go beyond the boundaries of North Austin. Its style was autocratic with little flexibility and it was quite incapable of engaging in dialogue.

But it was not designed to do any of these things. It was designed, rather, to be the religious and therefore, inevitably, the social and human center of the life of as many of the children and grandchildren of the immigrants as sought such a center. To judge it by the standards of a post-immigrant and post-Vatican Church is to engage in a narrowness even worse than that of St. Ursula. Whether the post-Vatican local Christian community will achieve *its* goals nearly as well as St. Ursula achieved the goals of the 1930s still must be very problematic.

I was proud of St. Ursula in the 1930s and can understand it in the 1970s. The religious worldview with which it equipped me was incomplete but I am still grateful for that worldview because it gave me a place on which to stand. And although it may have been incomplete, it was at least openended; it is extraordinarily difficult to *go* somewhere unless one is *from* somewhere; and I'm from St. Ursula.

But if there is little ambivalence in my emotions about St. Ursula there is, and always will be, extremely strong ambivalence in my feelings about St. Praxides for it was a religious experience

14

that remains in my bloodstream, I think to stay (if religious experiences can get into one's bloodstream). To say that it was the most important influence of my adult life is, if anything, to understate the case.

St. Praxides was another matter, quite different from St. Ursula. During the seven years I was in the seminary (1947-1954) a revolution occurred in the American Catholic population. We began to become members of the professional upper middle-class. St. Praxides was the fruit of that revolution. The first day I drove down the broad tree-lined streets of the parish, with its wide expanses of neatly manicured lawns surrounding large and gracious suburban homes, I knew I was in a different world from St. Ursula. My first view of the almost finished parish church, the first modern church in our diocese, confirmed my hunch that I was involved in a whole new ball game. I had been trained for a place like St. Ursula but I had been sent to a parish whose existence had completely escaped our seminary faculty. Small wonder, for St. Praxides represented the first large segment of the Catholic population of Chicago to make it into the ranks of the well-to-do. I am not sure whether it represented the last flowering of the immigrant Church or the first beginnings of the post-immigrant Church, or perhaps both; but even though my father was a business executive and, if he had lived, we probably would have moved to some place like St. Praxides, neither I, nor indeed anyone, was prepared for a parish made up almost entirely of college graduates.

The well-to-do suburban parish is now well known in American Catholicism; perhaps it is difficult to realize how untypical it was in the early 1950s. When one's view of the Church and the Church's mission in the United States has been shaped by a mentality that is proud of the fact that most of the faithful are "cap and seater people," one is taken aback by country clubs and Cadillacs, by suburban commuter trains, and real Notre Dame alumni instead of the subway variety. When only two or three of one's grammar school classmates have gone to college, one is caught

15

off guard seven years later by a community where it is expected that all high school graduates will go through college.

St. Praxides was the parish of the successful, well-educated business and professional men, their well-groomed, handsome and frequently neurotic wives, and their baffling, gifted, and frequently haunted children. I was warned about those children during my first weeks in the parish by everyone I talked to. The older priests, the nuns, the adult lay people all told me that the grammar school students and the teenagers were "spoiled rich kids" whose parents had given them everything, who had no respect for anybody or anything. In my decade there I searched diligently for these spoiled young people but found only one or two. All the others were, to a greater or lesser extent, intelligent, poised, respectful, and industrious. As a matter of fact, they were so sophisticated that it took me a long time to realize how much hollowness and self-rejection there was beneath the smooth veneer that they presented to the world.

Those European sociologists who flocked to the United States after the Second World War and were terribly upset by the fact that the American Catholic population was still going to church explained the high level of religious practice as a phenomenon of the national parish in the immigrant Church. Their confident prediction was that when the immigrant parish broke up and the children and grandchildren of the immigrants made it into the mainstream of American life, the levels of religious practice would fall to where they were in France. St. Praxides, then, was to be the place where the great drift away from Catholicism should begin. My European colleagues could not have been more wrong. Loyalty to the parish, enthusiasm over the Church—at least as it was perceived— generosity with time and money, commitment to every new project that the parish sponsored (be it the Christian Family Movement or bridge marathons) in St. Praxides made St. Ursula look quiet and stodgy by comparison. Instead of drifting away from the faith and the loyalty of their parents and grandparents, the third and fourth generation of Irish in St. Praxides had reached measures of religious behavior which I think have seldom been equaled in the long history of Christendom. Nor can the religious commitment of these well-to-do Catholic professionals be dismissed as mere culture religion, though surely it was very much a part of the culture of the neighborhood. It was a strange mixture of faith and boosterism, of tenacious clinging to the old combined with eagerness to find the new. We had the Sorrowful Mother novena and Cana conferences, the rosary during October and May, and the Gelineau psalms. Our pamphlet rack offered *Our Sunday Visitor* and *Commonweal.* There were people in the parish who never got beyond *Extension* and others who read *Cross Currents* and the *New Republic.* Some of our teenagers were involved in Father Lawlor's decent dress and decent disk crusades while others had the opportunity to talk with Godfrey Diekmann, Daniel Berrigan (in an earlier manifestation), and George Higgins, and not a few managed to encompass both the Left and the Right with equal enthusiasm. It was a community terribly afraid, one might even say obsessed, with the thought of Negro "immigration." Many of the people in the parish would rank high on any measure of social consciousness. And during the early 1960s, the era of John Kennedy and volunteerism, one authentically new lay movement (involving college students tutoring in the inner city) was born in St. Praxides.

St. Praxides had almost all that it takes—intelligence, enthusiasm, money, power, political and social leadership, and even, at least by the lights given it, religious commitment. Yet, there was something missing. It was not quite able to advance beyond the narrow bonds of suburban Irish respectability. This is not to say that there were not zealous and enthusiastic Christians at St. Praxides but it is to say that when the chips were down, when there were real opportunities either for individuals or for the community, one could never count on them. The community organization which, if it had worked, might have very well solved the problem of racial integration in the southwest side of Chicago, was torpedoed by suspicion and lethargy; and individual projects, especially among young people, would begin brilliantly, then gradually peter out, usually resulting in bickering and inefficiency. Parents inevitably stepped in to raise two of the most terrifying questions which could be asked in St. Praxides: "What will people say?" and "Who do you think you are?"

The ultimate reasons for this paralysis at the last moment, when faced with an opportunity and a challenge which was both human and Christian, are beyond the scope of this book. A dazzling, exciting, challenging, but ultimately depressing and discouraging place, the gloss of nostalgia does not blind me to the disappointments. I suppose it was foolish of one terribly energetic, but relatively naive young priest to think that he could turn St. Praxides around, to stir the South Side Irish out of their fear, their self-hatred, and their insidiously narrow respectability. I tried and I lost, and yet I must confess that if I had another chance I'd try all over again.

These, then, are my two basic experiences of church: a warm, stable, unexciting but supportive parish of childhood and a bedazzling, frustrating, obsessively fascinating parish of adulthood. The reader may not have quite as pleasant memories of his childhood parish nor quite so powerfully ambivalent feelings about the most important local church in his adult life, yet perhaps he begins to see what I mean. Both these experiences of church have precious little to do with infallibility, primacy, or any of the other arguments in the theology textbooks. They have very much to do with messy, complicated, primordial relationships which men and women fashion in that parish which is most meaningful in their life and in which they have invested the strongest commitments of their personality. Some will suggest that St. Praxides or St. Ursula were not *religious* in the sense that neither of them were "authentic, prophetic" communities, but this is a very narrow and *a priori* view of religion, a view which is quite isolated from the human condition. However, to the sociologist, a religious community is rather a group of people who share the same fundamental values about the most important things in their lives and gather together around this value system both to reinforce it by their unity and to share their lives with others whom they perceive to be, because of common values, "their kind of people."

In a previous volume I pointed out that one of the principal functions of religion was to provide man with a set of answers to the fundamental questions he must ask himself about the nature of reality. The other basic function of religion is to provide man with something to belong to, a community of those who share with him, however imperfectly, the responses to these basic questions. The local church is that community of fellow believers who are part of the place where we eat and sleep, live and love, raise our children, grow old and die. It is generally a physical place though occasionally it can be a psychic one. But it is a place where we belong to other people and they belong to us.

The most basic thing, then, that can be said about the local church is that it is people, not perfect people, not saints, not angels free from the grip of social class, ethnic group, geography, or culture, but rather men and women caught not merely in the human condition but also caught in that particular segment of time and place which has shaped their culture and their personalities. The perfectionists are scandalized by this. It is shocking and disgraceful that a group which claims to be God's people should be so time-bound and place-bound, and they are quite correct. But there is no way that a faith community made up of human beings can escape the time and space of which it is a part. If the Church is made up of people then it is also necessarily composed of creatures who are limited and finite. Therefore, it follows that since the Church is made up of people, it will always labor under imperfection and inadequacy; or, as the scripture says, the bride will be without blemish only when the bridegroom returns. In some sense, one supposes, the Church is infallible, but the local community includes in its membership only weak and fallible human beings.

This is a profound scandal to the perfectionists but our experience of Church tells us, if we are ready to examine that experience, that imperfection, weakness, fallibility, finitude are all part of the very nature of the Church, and will be eliminated only by eliminating people as its members.

Those of us who are used to beginning with a description of the Church that stresses its glories and its perfections are taken aback when someone starts his description of the Church with an insistence on the limitation which inevitably flows from the nature of its membership; and yet if we could reflect on our experience of Church and put aside the *a priori* dicta of the textbooks, the limitations and the imperfections of the Church look large in our experience. It is worth remembering that the Church described in the New Testament was also substantially less than perfect and that Jesus was quite explicit about his decision to bring his kingdom into being through the agency of the weak and the ignorant. When one looks around at the membership of the Church, be it either the members of the local community one knows best, or the leadership that one reads about, it is perfectly clear that the Lord's promise to work through the agency of the weak and the ignorant has not been violated. Of weakness and ignorance we do not have a shortage.

But one wonders whence comes the perfectionism. One hears from young enthusiasts today that if the Church does not eliminate all traces of "institutional racism," if it does not take an immediate stand for peace, then they will judge it to be "irrelevant" and leave it. Thirty years ago it was the cause of the trade unions that the Church was expected to dedicate itself to (a fact which would give the young enthusiasts pause if they ever bothered with such things as history). Again, we are told that the Church is irrelevant if it is not "poor" or "scientific" or "up-to-date" (which usually means rock music at Masses), or "committed to the Third World." In other words, the Church must be perfect now despite the fact that it has never been before, not even in the time of Jesus.

The call for the perfect Church is not new. It has been echoed by reformers down through history. Whether the reformers also became schismatics depended in great part on whether they insisted that the perfect Church be achieved instantaneously or whether they were willing to strive for it while awaiting fulfillment when the Lord returned. The sectarians who did break away found that the perfect Church they hoped to create soon suffered from all the imperfections of the old Church, but such a discovery did not prevent new generations of enthusiasts from rising up with the firm conviction that *they* could build the perfect Church.

The perfectionism of enthusiasts is even worse today. Knowing no history, raised in an atmosphere of triumphalism which led them to believe that the Catholic Church was virtually without flaw, they discovered to their horror that there was pettiness, inefficiency, venality, corruption, stupidity, ambition, greed, and hardness of heart within the Church. In other words, they discovered that it was made up of human beings who lived up to their own ideals very inadequately. To the youth of this and of every generation such a discovery is unacceptable.

I do not, therefore, apologize for the fact that St. Ursula and St. Praxides were imperfect. I apologize for the imperfections themselves and for the fact those those of us who were part of both communities did not strive with more enthusiasm to eliminate, or at least curtail the imperfections. I certainly apologize that we became complacent with the gap between what we aspired to be and what we were. I decry the provincialism of St. Ursula and the racism of St. Praxides, but because they were imperfect and flawed I do not thereby deny them the title of church. Quite the contrary, I assert that such fallibility and imperfection are a necessary part of our experiences of church and that no one who has ever experienced church has ever experienced one which is anything more than fallible and imperfect.

DON'T JUST GIVE ME ORDERS

THE idea that authority is the ability to give orders (an idea that is somewhat widespread among certain ecclesiastical leaders, and a portion of clergy and laity in the church today) is theologically, historically and sociologically naive. Right now we want to examine, from a historical and a sociological perspective, why practically, pragmatically, existentially, and empirically authority has to include the *ability to obtain consent.* The Lord Jesus himself could not get his apostles to do anything on which they had not agreed. Nor can the most oppressive totalitarian regimes govern without some kind of grudging consent. If the governed, if the subjects of authority, if those who must take orders deny the legitimacy of either the orders or the one who gives the orders, then, however theoretically valid and excellent the authority may be, it will practically and empirically have no effect at all.

The order-giving model of authority is still widespread in the church, not because it is soundly based theologically or historically, but rather because it was pragmatically functional for so many years. If a pope or a bishop or a pastor or even a priest gave an order, then it was normally obeyed because there existed a context of acceptance in which people were willing to give their consent to orders passed down by ecclesiastical authority. It is to be doubted that the order was always all that effective, but at least verbal dissent was rarely heard by the ordergivers themselves, however much moaning and groaning there may have been behind their backs. Peirre Teilhard de Chardin went along with the authority that ordered him to silence because he conceded legitimacy to such orders. Hans Kung does not because he does not concede such legitimacy. Athanasius never conceded the legitimacy of the various councils in the Eastern Mediterranean that denounced him, either.

The point of this line of reasoning is that order-giving authority functioned effectively not because of the power of the order giver, or not even necessarily because of the theological or historical grounds for such an approach, but because people were willing to consent to such an exercise of authority, a willingness which has not always existed in the past in the church and which patently does not exist now.

It may be argued that in the order-giving model of the exercise of authority things got done more quickly and effectively than they do now. When the ones in authority, like the bishop in our story, no longer gives orders, things have to be worked out in long tedious discussions in which the appropriate consent is obtained by other means. Still, in a complex world, order-giving only looks efficient. Consider the experience of the Germans in the Second World War and of the United States with the Viet Cong. Pragmatically and practically, the era of instant obedience to orders because the orders were conceded an instant legitimacy is over. If those in positions of authority in the Church wish to lead effectively, they must go back to old, more difficult, and yes, more political tactics to obtain consent. Whether this is a good or a bad thing may be debated; that it is necessary and inevitable is hardly open to debate. The practical question in the church now is not whether it is necessary to go through a lot of effort, formerly unneeded, to obtain consent, but rather, what kind of effort is appropriate and what matters are legitimate subjects for the quest for consensus.

From a sociological perspective we would say authority is the responsibility to influence human behavior, to motivate humans to behave in certain patterns. Also, it seems that anyone who has authority in the church is commissioned by God (or by divine delegate) to behave in such a way as to motivate Christians to behave in certain ways and especially to uncover the gospel ways to direct many of these behavior patterns. Indeed, it seems to us that this position is so reasonable as almost to be self-evident. There is, however, a certain kind of cleric (and some non-clerics) who become obsessively restless when such a suggestion is made. Those who hold this position are accused of trying to democratize authority or of trying to take away religious authorities' God-given powers.

To this we must say, even the most God-given powers have little impact in the world or on people's lives unless ways can be found to motivate them to respond to the wishes of those who may have that power. Also, it seems that for over a thousand years church authority was exercised through a deliberate attempt to obtain consent. Even Innocent III, that most imperious and imperial of the medieval popes, did not make decisions without obtaining the consent of the Roman cardinals. Also, for a millenium all major Christian doctrines were issued with something like "with the consent of the whole Christian people." We are not sure how that consent was obtained, but, at least theoretically, it was thought to be there. It seems that the order-giving approach to the theology of religious authority is a shallow theological rationalization for a renaissance model of government, which was a late-comer for the church and which has over-stepped its usefulness, such as it may have been. The order-giving model is ineffective and non-pragmatic. It is also bad theoretically.

Let us consider the approach of the sociologist to the problem of religious authority through an example: you can tell an altar boy to get to church at 6:30 and set up the sanctuary for 7:00 mass. But you can, by no means, guarantee his arrival unless you have motivated him to be there (quite probably you will also have to motivate his mother to get him out of bed so he can be there). A pastor can give orders until he is blue in the face to his associate pastors and other members of the parish staff. They in turn can give orders until they are similarly blue in the face (though to whom they would give these orders these days is open to question) and no one will follow them unless the ones who receive the orders are willing to respond, "All right, I will do it." Virtually the only power left in the hands of the ecclesiastical order givers, having sometime ago lost the secular arm, is the power of the paycheck. Once the clergy become financially independent, there will be no way the ecclesiastical authority can make them do something they have not agreed to do (Hans Kung might not be permitted to teach on the Catholic faculty, but he can still teach; and he is not about to stop calling himself a Catholic just because some people in Rome have decreed that he is no longer a Catholic theologian).

Unfortunately the model of authority as giving orders is firmly built into the structure of the church even though it has lost most of its effectiveness. Even those priests who were trained in the seminary over twenty-five years ago contested the pervasiveness of order-giving and were part of the covert but often highly effective resistence to it. The order-givers were able to maintain external control of human behavior but they were not able to control what people did after they were ordained—as the enormous number of priest resignations shows. Perhaps there is no greater indictment of the failure of order-giving as the model for ecclesiastical behavior than the large number of model seminarians who decamped from the priesthood despite their docility and obedience when they were in the seminary. All that keeps order-giving going successfully now in the church is the checkbook. It may once have been possible to treat the membership, be they priest or laity, as privates in the army. This is no longer possible and administrative disaster is the result of a continuation of such style.

There are at least three reasons why the order-giving model will not work in the church (at the local, diocesan, and world level) today.

1) First of all, this model assumes that the personnel beneath the order-giver are incapable of thinking for themselves. Even worse, it assumes that they are incapable of making a contribution of their own. The one who gives orders thinks he *knows* what must be done. It remains only for the subordinates to carry out those instructions. They have nothing of their own to contribute to the matter, no insight, no knowledge, no experience, that is of any importance at all. Yet, in fact, the people most familiar with the situation where a decision is to be implemented are those

who are actually the closest to the situation. He who governs by giving orders is deprived of the insights, the understanding, the recommendations and the human ingenuities of such people. He is governing, in effect, with one arm tied behind his back. . . . (the subordinate) is a cog in a machine and if you control him, he will be forced to act like a cog, at least until he can find another source of income. In fact, however, he will resent the treatment you have accorded him and will subvert your instructions whenever he can, not necessarily because he disagrees with your instructions, but because he sullenly resents being treated as though he were a sub-human tool. As we remember when we think of the pre-Vatican II seminary and as we consider authoritarian parishes even today, the one in the position of power may well give the instructions and impose external conformity, but the rank and file have a way of getting even by dragging their feet, by delaying, by putting spikes in the wheel, and by frustrating the authoritarianism of the leader. Remember John Kennedy during the Cuban missile crisis remarking, in astonishment, that he had ordered several months before that intermediate range ballistic missiles be removed from Turkey. "What are they still doing there?" he asked, not understanding the ability of the bureaucratic structure to resist an order of which they do not approve.

In 1980, Cardinal James Knox and the Congregation for the Sacred Liturgy issued a new set of liturgical regulations, most of which reaffirmed existing regulations (which, for the most part, had been ignored by those deeply involved in liturgical "reform"). The regulations dealt with peripheral problems such as communion under both species, communion in the hand, self-communication (a term that one man commented, "sounds like it must be a dirty word") and women servers. The proclamation did not deal with more fundamental questions like the loss of a sense of the transcendent and the bad taste, bad history, bad theology, bad art and music and bad pop liturgical wisdom which had come to be part of the Catholic liturgy. It simply gave orders. And as such, it was ignored in most places. Parishes where there were women servers continued to use them. The U.S. bishops responded only to complaints they received about liturgical violations realizing, as one bishop commented, "We tell them to stop and they say they will, but they don't." What is a bishop to do? Discontinue all liturgies?

3) Perhaps most important of all, the reasons against order-giving as a model for authority is the fact that, even with the best possible intentions, orders must be passed down through a chain of command and be reinterpreted, retranslated, reexplained, or at least re-transmitted at a number of communication links. A pastor tells an associate pastor something. He in turn tells the school principal; the principal tells the teachers; the teachers tell the kids. In all of these cases there may be sincere good will in transmitting what the pastor has said. But preconsciously, self-consciously, and unconsciously, the instruction is tailored, edited, and reshaped to suit what the transmitter takes to be the situation to which she is transmitting the order. It is a truism of research on hierarchical bureaucracy that orders are frequently, if not always, subverted as they are passed down the chain of command. Not out of malice (necessarily) but rather because with each new transmission there is a different perspective, a different understanding, and a different set of problems.

When one adds to this unconscious or subconscious subversion a deliberate intent to subvert, then the order-giver is in a most awkward situation. Pope Paul VI did issue his encyclical on birth control and right-wing Catholics can probably agree that it was a brilliant exercise of authority. In fact, bishops, confessors, theologians, parish priests, either consciously or unconsciously, but nonetheless very effectively, subverted the teaching of the encyclical. However it may clearly stand on the record as Paul's understanding of Catholic doctrine, it had no effect on human behavior, other than perhaps to turn Catholics against the church's teachings on sexuality. Is such an exercise of authority what is expected of a Christian leader?

Similarly, the Dutch Synod has been loudly cheered as a victory for conservative and law and order forces in the church. But it is reasonably clear that many of the Dutch bishops do not believe in its decisions, that the clergy believe in it even less, and that many of their people reject it completely. The synod then will not, in fact, restore order to the church in Holland, but simply increase the polarization. It will do so in part because there are people in the key links in the communication networks who are bent on destroying the effectiveness of the synod; but also because there are other people who may be less intent on deliberately subverting the synod but whose interpretation of what it means will in fact subvert the intentions of the Pope. An order-giving approach to authority, in other words, which does not engage in the enormously difficult task of winning consent, will not only not work, it is likely to be counterproductive. Perhaps one of the biggest problems faced by Pope John Paul II is that he still appears to believe that ecclesiastical authority enjoys the power it did for a certain time in Catholic history (though not the earliest times nor the longest times)—the ability to give orders without worrying about consent. Whatever the Pope may think, no parish priest or no bishop can afford the luxury of such self-deception.

If one defines authority more broadly (and probably more accurately, historically and theologically, as well as sociologically) as the responsibility to obtain consent, then we may still believe that authority comes from God (as we do), but we also realize that it has to be exercised in very different ways than that with which we became familiar in the church in recent decades and centuries. The person with authority must see himself charged with the responsibility to modify human behavior in the direction of the gospel by providing people with motivation other than the necessarily short run motivations of fear and force.

If one wishes to have any practical impact, then one must ask oneself what motivations are going to be effective in achieving such an impact. Practically speaking, the only approach that will work is the approach of asking challenging questions and providing a powerful vision of what the goals of the Church and Christian life are. The person who possesses effective authority is not the one who has the ability to give orders, but rather the one who has the ability to ask the most powerful and the most penetrating, most searching, most challenging questions—in part, by the way he behaves himself and in part by the direct and explicit questions he asks and in part by the kind of disconcerting, shattering "stories" he tells. In other words, Jesus' exercise of authority was much more effective because of the stories he told and the deeds he did than by the orders he gave which were, incidentally, few and far between. Washing the feet of the Apostles at the Last Supper was *the* lesson in the exercise of authority; and many churchmen seemed to have missed it, even though they may now go through the Last Supper rituals themselves at the Holy Thursday liturgy.

DID JESUS REALLY ESTABLISH THE CHURCH?

THERE is a church simply and solely because of the social aspect of human nature, because humans are gregarious creatures who cannot survive long by themselves. We need other human beings to be born, to be raised, to be loved, protected, educated, fed, clothed.

There are very few things we can do alone, and we certainly cannot effectively respond to the demand of a challenging religion by ourselves. We do not love by ourselves, we do not hope by ourselves, we do not care for others by ourselves; and so we do not worship, pray, nor respond to a God of love by ourselves.

The apostles did not sit around and say, "Should we have a church or not? Should we each do what the master told us without any organization? Should we each respond to the Easter experience of the risen Jesus in our secret hearts and not waste time and energy by setting up a structure?"

Nor did they say, "Let's sit down and make up a bunch of rules which 1900 years from now will be embodied in the code of canon law." They were a group of human beings who had been brought together by Jesus to hear his preaching, share his life, and to extend and continue his work. They continue to be a group of human beings doing their best at these tasks—and oftentimes, as we know, their best was not all that good—because it never would have occurred to them to proceed any other way.

Jesus did not found a church in the sense that he sat down one day and said, "All right, fellas, now we're going to start a church. Peter, I want you to go to Rome and open a savings account, a deposit of faith, into which you will enter all the things I've told you, and leave word for your successors to set up the College of Cardinals, write up the code of canon law. And I want the rest of you fellas to be bishops, set up diocesan curias and write pastoral letters and meet every once in a while at an ecumenical council to define doctrine. Having done that, you'll be a church. Oh, incidentally, Peter, you're going to be infallible, and the rest of you guys will be infallible, too, when you're with him.''

What Jesus did was gather together a group of people, preach to them, teach them, love them, and then send them forth to do his work. In that sense he founded a church. But then, of course, that is precisely the church we know very well in our local parish communities, a church which is in fact very much like the apostolic one—sometimes enthusiastic, sometimes disheartened, sometimes brilliant, sometimes disgraceful, sometimes generous, sometimes narrow, sometimes devout, sometimes missing the point completely, but always human, always straining for something beyond the human, always trying, however ineptly, to respond as best it can to the transhuman message that was revealed in Jesus and preached by him.

THE HIERARCHY AS SCAPEGOAT

THE word means either the organization of the Church in ascending grades of authority (a concept totally foreign to the gospel, though quite compatible with the Platonic philosophy of the era in which the Chruch emerged) or the leadership of the Church (and even in the gospel the Church quite clearly has leadership). The hierarchy is a marvelous scapegoat, an inkblot on to which we can project all our frustrations, the guilty party we can blame for everything that goes wrong. Heaven knows the American hierarchy has been monumentally undistinguished in the years since the Vatican Council—perhaps less so than it has been at any time in its history. But if the American Catholic clergy and laity are satisfied to be governed in some considerable part by mitred pinheads, then they deserve such leadership. On the other hand, it's always a lot easier to blame the hierarchy than to assume responsibility for creating renewed ideas and structures to bring new life to the Church. It is odd that often precisely those who talk most about freedom and initiative are also the ones most likely to scapegoat the hierarchy for the absence of new structures in the Church. In fact, the new Church will be built not in the chancery offices but at the grass roots, and to the extent that the new Church has failed to appear, the blame must be placed at the grass roots and not at the chanceries. It would still be nice, however, to have leaders who are intelligent, inspiring, sensitive, and sympathetic, compassionate and articulate instead of the dummies that many of us are saddled with. There are, of course, many able, intelligent, spiritually wise bishops. If you gave me some time I could maybe think of twenty.

THE "NEIGHBORHOOD" CHURCH
VS. THE CHURCH "DOWNTOWN"

WHEN the 1968 encyclical *Humanae Vitae* was issued there were two expectations of what the outcome would be. The right-wing expectation, confidently expounded by some Church leaders (perhaps many had their fingers crossed), was that the Holy Father had spoken, and those Catholics who were using birth control pills or other forms of contraceptives would stop. The left-wing expectation, heard in many liberal Catholic quarters, was that Catholics would continue to use birth control and leave the Church. While there has been a notable decline in religious devotion, there has not been an increase in disidentification from the Church because of the encyclical. The left and the right were both correct and incorrect. Catholics who practiced birth control did not leave the Church, but neither did they obey the Pope. They continued to practice birth control, according to liberal expectations, and stayed in the Church, according to conservative expectations. Both sides would consider them inconsistent, but such inconsistency does not seem to bother the ordinary Catholic lay person. In addition, then, to alienation, dissatisfaction and disidentification (about which more in a subsequent chapter), there is also another way of sorting out one's relationship with a religious denomination. One could call this form of dissidence "voluntarism."

By "voluntarism" I do not mean that church membership is voluntary. There being no established church in this country and no real inheritance of religious affiliation, church membership for American Catholics has been voluntary since its very beginning. I mean, rather, that American Catholics have discovered that it is possible to be a Catholic in the way one chooses, without regard for the "official" norms of Catholic behavior, as these are imposed either by the teaching Church through its hierarchical rep-

33

resentatives or by the elite, liberal Church through bureaucratic agencies and journalistic media.

I have used the models of "communal Catholic" and "the two churches" before to emphasize different aspects of this new voluntarism. The communal Catholic model suggests that many Catholics choose to be Catholics the way many Jews choose to be Jews: that is, they identify with the Catholic community, are interested in the Catholic heritage and tradition, wish to pass Catholicity on to their children, but do not look to the Church for meaningful instructions on how to regulate their lives. Some communal Catholics are devout, others not; but the critical point is that even the non-devout have no inclination to identify as anything else but Catholic and the devout have little inclination to yield much credibility to the Church as an official teacher.

My "two-church" model was proposed as an alternative to the two-church view of those who see one church as the bureaucratic hierarchy and the other as the liberal laity. I contend that a much more useful model compares the Church in the "neighborhoods" with the Church "downtown." The neighborhood Church is the Church at the parish level and beneath; the downtown Church is of the chancery office and above. Whether it be the Church of the conservative hierarchical bureaucracy *or* the Church of the liberal elites, the neighborhood Church doesn't pay much attention to either. It asks only that the downtown Church leave it alone. It does not look to the hierarchical Church downtown for guidance on birth control, and it does not look to the liberal Church downtown for guidance on racial attitudes and social problems. It pays little attention to either the *National Catholic Reporter* or *The Register,* either to *The Commonweal* or *Our Sunday Visitor,* either to the Washington and Chicago meetings of bishops or the Detroit meetings of the liberation theologians and the Call to Action. In fact, it is barely aware that these exist.

Essential to both these models is the assumption that a substantial proportion of the Catholic population is no longer listening to communications from elite levels, whether they be hierarchical or liberal intellectual. In both cases the rank and file Catholic either ignores or explicitly rejects the right of the elite to tell him or her what to do and how to live. Compliance with elite norms and directives, in other words, is part of the voluntary component of church affiliation.

The second assumption of both models is as critical as the first. The "communal" Catholic is free to affiliate or not to affiliate. When he affiliates he does so on terms of his own choosing, with little concern for the alleged inconsistency with which he is charged by the downtown elites. The failure of communication between downtown and the neighborhood is so complete that the neighborhood not only no longer listens to downtown, it even denies the *right* of downtown to establish norms.

A series of questions in the NORC Catholic schools study asked respondents whether the Church had the right to teach what position Catholics should take on certain issues. The two issues considered here are racial integration and birth control. The answers to these questions correlated at a sufficiently high level (.39) that they can be formed into an index called "communal Catholic."

Of the Catholics in the country, 85 percent reject the Church's right to teach on one or the other issue; 49 percent reject its right to teach on both them. Half the Catholics in the United States, in other words, deny the Church has the right to lay down what position Catholics should take on "proper means of family limitation" and "racial integration." The first of our two assumptions fits the data nicely. Half the American Catholic population has turned off the "downtown" Church on both the "liberal" issue of racial integration and the "conservative" issue of birth control.

What impact does such a decision to reject the legitimacy of the Church's teaching have for these "neighborhood communal Catholics"? . . . Neither in their background nor in their observable religious practice is there much difference between those Catholics who accept the teaching authority of the Church and those who reject it. However theologically and philosophically inconsistent it may be, a very substantial proportion of the Catholic population (about half) is able to reject ecclesiastical authority's right to teach authoritatively on race and on birth control and still maintain approximately the same levels of religious practice as do the general Catholic population.

One suspects that this finding will be greeted with disbelief and perhaps contempt by both the right-wing and the left-wing elites. As one Roman cardinal said to me, "It is too bad they don't have the faith anymore." And as a Pittsburgh monsignor said to me, "We are ashamed of Catholics in the ethnic neighborhoods." Shameful and unfaithful they may be, but apparently they don't realize it. They reject the Church's right to teach on birth control and race and still continue their routine Catholic behavior almost entirely unaffected by such rejection of teaching authority.

How can such inconsistency occur? First of all, one must note that there is no evidence at all that the people engaging in communal Catholic behavior think that they're being inconsistent. They obviously do not think that it is necessary for devout Catholicism to accept the Church's right to authoritatively teach on racial and sexual matters. Elite Catholicism may say, "But you have to accept our right to tell you what you should think about sex and/or race." It is the essence of voluntarism that the communal Catholic can respond, "That's what *you* say." You have your official models of Catholic behavior, in other words, and I have mine, and you can't make me live according to your model.

There has been a substantial increase in the number of communal Catholics since the first NORC study in 1963 (rising from 30 percent of the population to 50 percent). As in most other matters reported in *Catholic Schools in a Declining Church*, virtually all the increase in the number of communal Catholics can be accounted for by a decline in support for papal authority and a decline in endorsement of the Church's official birth control teaching (and none of it relates to the support for the changes in the Second Vatican Council). My colleagues and I concluded in *Catholic Schools in a Declining Church* that the dramatic decline in Catholic religious practices seem to be affiliated with the birth control encyclical *Humanae Vitae* (there was considerable supporting evidence from other data sets for this conclusion). It now also appears that the fundamental explanation for the increase in the number of communal Catholics is the reaction of a large proportion of the Catholic population to *Humanae Vitae*—a reaction which seems to have caught both the left-wing and the right-wing elites off balance. The right-wing elites predicted that once the Pope had spoken, the matter would be closed, and Catholics would abandon artificial birth control. The left-wing elites predicted that once the Pope had spoken, Catholics would leave the Church and continue to practice birth control. In fact, both were wrong: Catholics continued to practice birth control and stayed in the Church (for the most part). The principal effect seems to be declining levels of religious devotion, and an increase of those who reject the Church's right to be an authoritative teacher.

One should ponder for a moment that three-quarters of those who reject the Church's right to teach authoritatively on race and on birth control are still willing to increase their annual contribution for the support of a de facto exercise of the Church's teaching function in the Catholic schools, and that half are willing to give fifty dollars and more a year to support the exercise of that function in their parish. It is all right, in other words, it would seem, for the Church to teach, but in certain areas of the exercise of the teaching authority, the Church no longer seems to enjoy any *credibility* as a teacher. One may speculate, in the absence of data, that a substantial number of Catholics in the United States simply do not think the Church is believable when it speaks on race or sex because it is their impression that the Church does not know what it's talking about: It does not understand the problems of marital intimacy and child rearing; it does not understand the problems of racially changing neighborhoods, of urban crime, of deteriorating schools, inflation, increasing taxes and decline of governmental services. If people have made up their minds that you do not know what you're talking about, you can talk until you are blue in the face and you will have no impact at all. You can claim to speak for God, or, alternatively, for the enlightened Christian conscience. The implicit response from the communal Catholic is that God knows what He's talking about but you don't, so why should he believe you are speaking for Him? One may insist until Judgment Day that one is speaking for God, but if people deny that basic assumption, they will simply tune you out and turn you off.

WHY HAS ECUMENISM FAILED?

I don't think Ecumenism has failed at all. On the contrary, I think it has been an enormous success. In the space of a relatively few decades the Reformation and the Counter-Reformation have been brought to an end, and Catholics, Protestants, Jews and others are now talking to one another like friends, brothers and sisters, men and women of good will (except perhaps in Northern Ireland). This is fantastic progress and we should rejoice in it. If you mean by "failure" the fact that ecumenism has not eliminated denominational differences or has not yet produced a "super church," then a couple of points might be made.

1) There are still doctrinal and cultural differences among the denominations. Doctrinal differences could take a long time to work out even though considerable progress has been made in ecumenical conversations at the theological level. There was perhaps an unrealistic expectation in the years immediately after the Vatican Council that all these differences would go away. It has been relatively easy for Catholics and Anglicans and Orthodox, and even Lutherans, for example, to achieve broad doctrinal consensus. For Baptists and Fundamentalists, there is a long, long way to go and the discussions have only just begun.

2) It is not at all clear that the cultural differences ought to go away. One would hate, for example, to see the strong, vigorous piety of the Lutheran Church of Missouri Synod or the marvelous gospel music of the Baptist Church be blunted and absorbed out of existence. It may be that the proper model for ecumenism is not a super church but rather loose denominational cooperation in which the denominations come closer together in doctrine and in practice and in friendship and still maintain their authentic cultural and historical differences. The super church endeavors in

the past have almost always failed and indeed ended up producing more, rather than fewer, denominations.

3) The Roman Curia does not want a church unity of any sort. Its recent torpedoing of the results of many years of work in the Roman Catholic Anglican dialogue indicates that the Curia does not want any other denomination hanging around Rome threatening its own power. There are very, very few differences (women's ordination being one of them) that prevent formal unity between Canterbury and Rome. But an Anglican presence within the broad Catholic community would be an enormous threat to the monopoly on power that the Roman Curia holds and curial bureaucrats are simply not about to give that power up.

Despite these factors, however, the peace and the friendship and the cooperation among various denominations is a wonderful development. It happened more quickly than anyone would have thought possible and hence there is now some breathing space before we move on to the next phase, a phase whose precise direction is not yet clear. But the pause comes not from failure but from tremendous success.

Chapter Two

You Are a Priest, Forever!

TODAY'S PRIEST: UNSURE AND ARROGANT

THE present state of the priesthood is marked by two pervasive conditions:

1) A loss of nerve among many priests as a result of the failure of confidence in the importance and uniqueness of their work.

2) An attempt to capture some importance for their vocation by redefining themselves as social activists instead of religious leaders.

As a result of these two situations, the conventional wisdom is that the priesthood of the future will be very different from the priesthood of the past. In years to come, it is said, the typical priest will be a part-time, married worker, ordained by the people of his community and he, in all likelihood, will be a she. The institutional church, like the socialist state, will wither away, and the part-time, married women priests responsible only to the local congregation will be the characteristic Catholic clergy.

Such was the vision of the priesthood espoused by the sometime Monsignor Ivan Illich in an article in *The Critic* many years ago, an article which had influence in notable disproportion to its intelligence. Illich's vision of the priesthood is both bad theology and bad sociology. Since, however, most of the leaders of the American priesthood—delegates to the meetings of the National Federation of Priests' Councils and the conference of major religious superiors of men—do not know much theology or sociology, the myopic and minimalist vision of the future of the priesthood is likely to continue. In fact, however, the future of the priesthood will be very different from what these blind men, who are leaders of the blind, imagine. One does not project into the future from a trend line established five years ago. Rather one projects from a much longer historical base. Such projection, of course, is impossible for those who are even more illiterate about history than they are about theology and sociology. Nevertheless,

43

if one wants to know what priests will do in the twenty-first century, then one must ask what priests did in the first century, the eleventh century, the seventeenth century, the nineteenth century, and the early twentieth century. If one asks those questions and investigates those base points, then one would conclude that the priesthood of the future will be very much like the priesthood of the past—for the most part, made up of full-time, unmarried men (and perhaps, eventually, full-time, unmarried women).

The theological grounds for the loss of nerve among priests are to be found in the mistaken conviction of some theologians that the only way one can persuade the laity of their religious importance is by restraining and minimizing the role of the clergy. There has grown up since the Vatican Council a theology of the priesthood (with little in the way of historical documentation) that reduces the priest to a Mass-sayer and an absolution-giver, and virtually eliminates his long historical role as the religious leader of the community. In fact, a more careful study than that in which these theologians have engaged would even eliminate the need for a priest as an absolution-giver, since the laity gave absolution for at least 1300 years of Catholic history.

This minimalist theology, practiced even by such greats as Edward Schillebeeckx and Hans Kung, has had tremendous appeal among the anti-clerical lay pseudo-intellectuals who dominate liberal Catholic journals and minister in turn to the self-hatred of the clergy. It has also been reinforced by the emergence of the so-called "new ministries" in Catholic life—youth minister, director of religious education, etc., etc., etc. With "youth ministers" and "DRE's" and "parish staffs," the typical nerve-losing parish clergyman says, "There's nothing left for us to do, nothing distinctive but our robes, we are a vanishing breed."

Under such circumstances, it is understandable perhaps that priests through their national leaders turn to the cheap grace of instant social action militantism. Thus, establishing the truth of Greeley's (Third) Law: There is an inverse relationship between the vitality of an institution and the militancy of its social action rhetoric. This law, which also can be called the law of Catholic organizations, can be rephrased simply as "the more relevant the rhetoric, the more irrelevant the organization," and can be expressed even more bluntly with the following words: certain evidence that an institution is about to liquidate itself is that those presiding over the liquidation will inform leaders of other institutions how to resolve their problems.

Thus, the conferences of major superiors of men assembles at a time of the greatest crisis in Western Catholic religious life since St. Benedict and passes ringing resolutions against the neutron bomb, the defense budget, Reagan economics, and American involvement in El Salvador, and vigorously endorses both gun control and the ERA.

No one in his/her right mind would think that these long lists of militant resolutions would change the vote of one congressman or even the mind of one Catholic. Indeed, they won't even change the mind of one member of the religious communities represented at the meeting. But they do provide the religious leaders with a way of feeling good as the walls come tumbling down around them. Vocations, direction, morale, vision—all of these apparently are to be ignored if only one can equate the work of one's Holy Founder with contemporary, social action fads. The successors of Francis and Dominic and Ignatius and Benedict and Jean Jacques Ollier have been reduced to repeating the warmed-over cliches of year-old editorials in the *Nation* or the *Christian Century* or the *Washington Post*.

And their counterparts at the National Federation of Priests' Councils, having been told that the most important influence on the religious life of Catholics is the quality of Sunday preaching, and that 80 percent of the Catholics in the country gave the clergy low marks on preaching, wanted to talk not about how they improve the quality of their homily, but rather about the problems of Latin America. As one priest, in as sublime a statement as one can imagine of the idiocy currently affecting the presbyterate, put it, "The whole world is my parish, not merely the people that listen to me on Sunday."

It did not occur, apparently, to this absurd man that he had little chance of influencing the whole world and considerable chance of influencing his parishioners. Nor that his parishioners pay his salary so that he minister the word of God to them. Nor that having failed in his obligation of strict justice to preach the Gospel well to them, he was a hypocrite, a whitened sepulchre if he preached about justice anywhere else in the world.

In the short run, the blind fools will remain with us and will do a tremendous amount of harm. They may indeed be responsible for the liquidation of the religious orders of men in the United States as we now know them and for a considerable diminishment of the size of the diocesan presbyterate. However, with no understanding of the past and no comprehension of the present, these men at best will have a negative influence on the future. They are lost explorers perishing in the wilderness instead of the pioneers of the new humanity as they imagine themselves.

I will leave to others the refutation of the naive theology of the priesthood which creates what passes for virtue in the contemporary American presbyterate, and content myself with sticking to my own loom of social science.

First of all, the priesthood is the only profession that I know of that tries to define itself not only without any regard for those who are its role opposites, but indeed without considering that any useful input at all might be made by the ordinary clergy. Priests are what priests say they are and the laity had damn well better be satisifed with that. In fact, all the empirical evidence shows that the laity still regard priests as religious leaders and still want full-time priests, preferably (though not necessarily) celibate. The data also show the enormous importance in the religious life of the church of such traditional priestly activities as preaching and counseling and finally demonstrate that when the clergy begin to preach about social justice—their newest amusement—the laity promptly turn them off because of their conviction that on such matters the clergy are not better informed or no more useful as guides than they are when they speak about the rules appropriate for married sexuality.

The priest, in other words, is as important as he ever was in the church, and probably more important because the laity look much less to the bishops and to the pope for leadership than they did twenty years ago. Indeed, the most important people in the religious life of a Catholic lay person are that person's spouse and that person's parish priest—note well, not youth ministers, or directors of religious education, or any of the other currently fashionable additions to the parish staff. If priests want to believe that their ministry is less important because of the development of the ''new ministry'' and because of the emergence of a new theology of the laity, there is nothing much that one can do to change that belief. At least they ought to be told, insistently and repeatedly, in season and out of season, that there is extremely powerful empirical evidence to the contrary.

How can it be that the laity, who pay the bills, can have such a completely different picture of the importance of priestly ministry and of traditional priestly occupations such as preaching and counseling than do priests themselves?

Part of the answer to this question, I am convinced, is the arrogance of priests. I use the word arrogance here in a carefully delimited sense: the assumption by priests that because they are priests they know all that there is to know and all they need to know on any given subject. The old a priori scholastic, philosophical and theological training in the seminary produced a presbyterate which thought it knew the answer even before the questions were asked. Scholasticism is dead but the serene self-confidence of the poorly educated clergyman that his own random ideas picked up on the morning news are the final word on almost any given subject has been little changed. There are few if any feedback mechanisms built into priestly ministry, not even a wife to tell you when you are making a damn fool out of yourself. Therefore, when a priest talks nonsense, he is likely to be greeted with silence (sometimes sullen silence, but after a while a priest becomes so insensitive to reactions to his foolishness that he doesn't even note how sullen the silence is). While priests have militantly advocated channels of communication by which they may speak upward to the bishops and the pope, they have paid little attention to building channels of communication beneath themselves through which the laity may express their view of things. In such a set of circumstances, then, the priest listens to those laity to whom he wants to listen and thus guarantees that his prejudices, preconceived opinions, and ridiculous biases are confirmed even before he listens.

Moreover, the changes in the church have by no means eliminated the authoritarianism of the clergy. Most priests still believe that they are the "boss" and since most people in the parish have better things to do than fight the parish priest, the pastor can still do pretty much what he wants. And indeed the modern, authoritarian, tyrannical pastor may even be more powerful than his predecessor because he has all the tricks of psychological gimmickry available to facilitate manipulation.

Thus, one of the finest parishes in the country was destroyed in a month by a new pastor who said all the right things but who drove teenagers from the rectory, dictated what kind of clothes women should wear, lengthened the parish liturgy, and eliminated popular priests from the parish staff—all while mouthing the most approved pseudo-liberal cliches. He could get away with it of course because he had the piece of paper in his pocket from the chancery office. He was the pastor. It was his parish. He owned it, and he could do anything he damned well pleased. The authoritarianism and arrogance, then, of the clergy frees them from any need of listening to what the laity really need and want in their parish ministers. The fool who destroyed this parish was convinced that his role was to be the man who brought order and discipline and administered integrity to the community. The people wanted what they had had and what all the people wanted—priests who speak inspiringly and console sympathetically. But no one asked them, and no one is likely to ask them.

Sometimes I am convinced that the clergy do not want to hear of the importance of preaching and counseling because they know how bad they are at it and are afraid that they are incapable of improving. It is much easier to be an authoritarian administrator or a peace and justice pietist than it is to be a good preacher and a kind and sympathetic counselor.

What then will the priesthood of the future be like? If the laity have any say about it—and, since they pick up the bills, eventually they will—the priesthood of the future will be marked fundamentally and essentially by an enormous improvement in the quality of preaching and the quality of sympathetic listening. The arrogant, authoritarian administrator will be replaced by men (and, please God, women) who know how to listen sympathetically, encourage sensitivity, preach effectively, and console lovingly. There may not be much difference between this ideal of the priesthood and that which has existed for almost two thousand years. Indeed, its "old fashioned" aspect may discourage and depress and even affront those who are convinced that that which is new is good and that which is old can't possibly be good. Nonetheless, as a sociologist, I must state candidly and bluntly that the preacher and the consoler, the poet and the precinct captain are what the laity want in their clergy, and I cannot imagine them not getting what they want eventually—although the clergy's capacity to preach justice for everyone else in the world and not practice justice towards their lay people is so profoundly structured into the priestly worldview that the presbyterate may be able to hold off its employers for a considerable period of time.

Will there be no structural changes at all? Will priests in 2082 be doing pretty much the same thing that priests did in 1082?

I'm inclined to answer that there will be rather few structural changes and that indeed 2082 will look remarkably like 1082. People will still go to priests for challenge and consolation. Priests will still preside over the liturgy and preach the word of God, and priests will still be the religious and to some extent the social leaders of the Catholic community.

There may be some institutional changes. Hopefully there will be women priests. But I do not believe that the ordination of women will affect the structure of the ministry any more than the extension of the vote to women affected the structure of politics. In both cases, the changes are matters of justice but not institutionally transformative.

There are, however, two structural changes which seem to me to be worth mentioning: a much closer interaction on a social, personal and human basis between the clergy and the laity; and the development, first *de facto* and then *de jure,* of a limited service priesthood.

The conventional wisdom since the second Vatican Council has been that the priest ought to emerge from the secluded protection of the rectory and become a human like other humans. As my students at the University of Arizona have put it, "a priest should be as human as we are so he can understand all the problems that we suffer; but he should be a little bit better at dealing with those problems so that he can give us a model to imitate." The author of the Epistle to the Hebrews could not have put it better.

However, neither the clergy nor the laity have thought through, or indeed have thought at all about the problems of the heightened vulnerability of the priest once he becomes no longer the odd man in the rectory but the odd man out, the stranger, the third man, the one who does not fit in the ordinary life of the community. Since I believe that celibacy is likely to continue, I see the priest-as-odd-person to be a very serious problem for himself and for his lay people until both sides are prepared to accept it and even rejoice in the priestly oddity. However, at the present time, all too many laity will insist, on the one hand, on the need for human interaction with priests, and on the other be threatened and terrified if the priest continues to be disconcerting; that is to say, if he continues to be an eschatological witness to a world beyond this one and to a reality which transcends this one.

Most lay people, it seems to me, are perfectly delighted with lap-dog priests that they can patronize and protect and dominate, but they don't want strong, tough priests who minister a gospel of paradox and challenge. By what they say, by what they do, and by who they are, a very substantial number of the clergy, it would seem, are only too content to settle down to be domesticated pets who disconcert only with radical social action rhetoric which, of course, has no practical effect on peoples' lives.

One is reminded of the famous remark of novelist Bruce Marshall to the Harvard intellectual who complained about the Irish priest in Boston. The clergyman, it seems, preached mostly on sexual sin and rarely mentioned the sins of concentration camps, to which Marshall replied that not very many members of the parish in question were likely to commit a concentration camp—similarly not many laity are likely to commit a neutron bomb or a multinational corporation. Hence, radical social action rhetoric is not likely to be disconcerting to them at all.

The priest as-odd-person-out is one of the deepest, most painful problems facing the church today and one which no one is willing to face, indeed, even address. Eventually, in the priests of the future, it will have to be faced.

Moreover, it seems likely that we will have in the years ahead a limited service priesthood. I do not mean the part-time priest who so delights Msgr. Illich and his admirers. I mean a full-time priesthood for a limited period of a person's life. A young man or a young woman will agree, for example, to commit five years of their life to the ministry of the priesthood (which will continue to be celibate). At the end of that period, they and church leaders will reconsider and another period of commitment might or might not be made. Precisely because one need not plan to be a priest until one dies, a much larger number of young people will experiment with a priestly career, and many of them, finding it both satisfying and challenging, will remain priests for a long period of time, if not indeed for their whole life and the result will be a much larger presbyterate than we have now and a solution to the priest shortage.

There are theological objections to this development, most of which seem to miss the point: that if one indeed is a priest forever, one need not be committed to the active exercise of the ministry forever. Such a permanent commitment to the priesthood in most eras before the last century probably only meant ten or fifteen years at the most, on the average. Now it means fifty years on the average. The church has not been able to comprehend the enormous difference that this demographic change makes and refuses to reflect on its theological implications.

However, practically do we not indeed have a limited term priesthood? The young men who are ordained in the 1980s know full well that leaving the priesthood is socially and religiously acceptable, if canonically somewhat more difficult than it was a few years ago. However, since few people take canon law seriously anymore, John Paul II's restrictions in granting dispensations from the priesthood are not likely to have much effect. We have, in other words, all the disadvantages of a limited service priesthood, with none of the recruiting advantages. I cannot imagine such a situation lasting for very long. So, entering the priesthood or leaving it could easily become a relatively simple career change and one which would greatly benefit the life of the church.

That's why nobody wants to talk about it presently. Much better to rant about the neutron bomb.

I should make clear by way of concluding parenthesis that I don't like the neutron bomb. As a matter of fact, I don't like the machine gun or gun powder either. I believe that in the future, priests will preach on social justice even as they did in the past. I trust that this future social justice preaching will be based, as it was in the past, on a far clearer understanding of the unique Catholic social theory which those who go to the NFPC and the CMSM meetings seem to have forgotten completely. I also presume that such deep and passionate concern, which has always marked the priesthood, for the poor and the oppressed of the world will not in the future be used, as it now is, as an excuse for not performing one's own professional obligations well. Priests in the future, I would submit, will rediscover that people will take them seriously when they speak about social concerns if they themselves are concerned about justice in their own ministry.

My emphasis then in this chapter is not against social action ministry in the future of the priesthood, but rather in favor of social action ministry that is professionally competent and well informed, that is steeped in traditional Catholic social theory and that is not a quick and easy substitute for the daily responsibilities of pastoral work—social action ministry, in other words, that is not "cheap grace."

The view of the priesthood expressed here is unfashionable and will, I fear, be unpopular, since it emphasizes continuity rather than change, tradition rather than revolution, a priestly ministry with which we are all familiar instead of one spun out of cotton-candy fantasies. Any serious and responsible consideration, it seems to me, of the trend lines set by the past and the present of the priesthood can only project a future in which priests will be doing pretty much what they've always done. This is not necessarily a conservative perspective, but an honest one.

WHY IS THE PRIESTHOOD
A PERMANENT STATE?

THE old answer used to be because in the sacrament of orders
a permanent "character" is placed on the soul of the priest.
Exactly how a character can be placed on the soul was something
that preconciliar theology never bothered to explain.

In the years after the Council, however, I think a number of
theologians went to the other extreme and argued, in effect, that
the priesthood was only a transient state, a temporary deputation
by the local community which loses its validity when the local
community withdraws the deputation.

I do not want to engage in theological controversy which is beyond my competence, but I will say that the more recent mini-
malistic descriptions of the priesthood are sociological nonsense.
Once a man is set aside for those things that pertain to God, that
act of having been set aside is something which becomes a characteristic of his personality (and it was probably the recognition
of this characteristic which led originally to the "character"
theology). You can no more eliminate the fact that you were once
deputed to mediate between God and humankind than you can
obliterate the color of your eyes, the shape of your skull, or even
your skin color and your sexuality. A priest is a priest is a priest
is a priest in virtually every culture that humankind knows. It may
be altogether possible and indeed even acceptable and virtuous
for a man to exercise the function of presiding over the Eucharistic
and the religious community only for a certain period in his life.
But the fact that he once played that role can no more be eliminated
from his biography than can the fact that a man was a general in
the Air Force or an all-American fullback—and for those defenders
of the old character theology who think that being an all-American
fullback is an "accidental" phenomenon, one simply has to say

that they don't read the sports pages or watch television or understand what it means to be, let us say, a Heisman trophy winner.

In other words, the priesthood is a permanent state for the same reason that being a Heisman trophy winner is a permanent state—it's something that when it happens to you it's so important, it's always part of you for the rest of your life, no matter what else you may do.

WHY HAVE SO MANY PRIESTS AND NUNS ABANDONED THEIR VOCATIONS?

FIRST of all, we must say that most priests and most nuns have not abandoned their vocations. The majority have remained loyal. Indeed, for priests, the resignation rate is substantially lower than the divorce rate for Catholic marriages.

Most of those who left the priesthood (and I can speak with confidence on this subject because of research my colleagues and I at the National Opinion Research Center have done) were simply not happy in doing the work of priests. In the absence of happiness in one's work, the loneliness of the celibate life becomes intolerable. It is worth noting that the majority of them would not return to the priesthood even if they could do so as married priests, and only 20 percent of them would return to the work they had been doing if they could do so as married priests. (The others would want weekend work or specialized kinds of work.) Thus 80 percent of the resigned priests are really not interested in going back to the sort of work they had been doing. Were men and women any less unhappy in their religious life before the Second Vatican Council? I doubt it. But the Council and the subsequent changes in the church, as well as the vacilitating and erratic but nonetheless authentic sympathy of Pope Paul VI for unhappy priests, made it much easier for priests to obtain dispensations, and once it became easy canonically to leave the priesthood, it was discovered that lay people were sympathetic towards resigned priests, not hostile, and that even the families of resigned priests could accept their resignation with some equanimity. So when, more recently, dispensations became harder to get, the attitude in the Catholic community toward the resigned priest continues to be sympathetic and many men will leave the priesthood and marry even though they do not have a dispensation because they feel that God and the Catholic community will be sympathetic and tolerant even if the papacy is not.

On the whole, even though I sometimes feel abandoned when a priest I know leaves the active ministry, I guess I have to say that both the church and the person are better off and that keeping men in the priesthood who are fundamentally and profoundly unhappy is no help to the service of human-kind or the preaching of the gospel.

Where the church and the religious orders might be to blame for some of the unhappiness in the men and women who elect to leave is, I think, a very important question. Clearly the religious life, for example, was extremely constrained and indeed sometimes intolerably oppressive for many women. The constraints and the oppressions have little to do with Christianity and indeed were, if anything, in violation of the spirit of the gospel. It is not clear, however, whether the hasty reforms in the religious communities after the Vatican Council were an adequate response to these problems. Indeed, the changes made may have done more harm than good and may have thrown the baby out with the bath water— though, as an outsider to the religious life, I cannot say this for certain. Surely the feudal domination of curates by pastors was a horrendous situation which the church tolerated far too long (and to some extent still tolerates today), and the autocratic Renaissance Monarch Bishop, though a vanishing breed, also made many men's lives virtually intolerable. Without wishing to take away the personal responsibility of those who elect to leave the priesthood or religious life, I nonetheless must say that I think their resignations are a judgment on the institutional church for its inability to make the priesthood and the religious life much more livable than they were and to some extent still are.

THE VOCATION PROBLEM

THE vocation problem is a priest problem and not a young person problem. Paradoxically, it would appear that precisely at a time when the preaching and counseling abilities of priests are most important to Catholics, priests themselves have relatively little regard for the importance of their own work. Though American Catholics may complain about the quality of preaching and the quality of counseling and sensitivity they encounter in the rectory, they still have considerable respect for the sincerity and the diligence, if not the professional competence, of their priests. While many of them, and among the young adults most of them, think that priests are too authoritarian and still expect the laity to be followers rather than colleagues or leaders and while about half of them object to priests becoming too involved in politics, the admiration and respect and affection for parish priests was still high. Moreover, the most powerful single influence in facilitating the return of someone to the church who had drifted away—particularly a young Catholic in early and middle twenties—was a relationship with a priest.

Preaching, counseling, close relationships with young adults, are at least as important in the church of the late seventies and of the early eighties as they were in the church before the Vatican Council. And yet, the overwhelming majority of young Catholics have no contact with and indeed no opportunity to establish contact with priests. Priests, in other words, are at least as important in the lives of the lay people as they used to be. But unfortunately, perhaps because of poor communication with lay people, they do not seem to have as much confidence in the importance of their own ministry as they had in the years before the Second Vatican Council. And because of that lack of conviction of their own importance and of the future importance of their work, they are disinclined to invite other young men to follow them into the

58

priesthood. The decline is not in the importance of priestly ministry but rather, it would seem, in priestly perception of the importance of their own ministry. On the basis of the somewhat meager data available to us it is reasonable to speculate that the clergy continue to have an enormous crisis of morale, a crisis created by the change in the Vatican Council, aggravated perhaps by the euphoria and then disillusionment in the five years after the council and made still worse by the defection from the active ministry of between a fifth and a quarter of the priests in the country, and made yet worse by the conviction, not supported by facts, that the work of the priesthood is no longer important to the religious life of the laity.

Precisely at a time when the quality of Sunday preaching is a powerful predictor both of the strength of religious affiliation and of the development of the religious imagination, and when contact with the priest is the most important element in a young person's drift back to the church after he or she has drifted away, precisely at this point it would seem, priests are at least as important in the lives of lay people as they used to be.

MARRIED PRIESTS?

THREE-QUARTERS of the American Catholic population could live with the notion of a married clergy, and two-thirds actively support a married clergy—quite likely because they believe the Church would change its teaching on birth control and be more sensitive to the problems of married people if its clergy were married. In fact, however, clergy are as much opposed to the birth control teaching of the Church as are the laity; the problem does not lie in clerical insensitivity but in curial insensitivity. Nevertheless, the laity would certainly not be shocked at having married priests—though they might be shocked at having to pay them and to concede to them the private lives that married men require (and which Protestant ministers and their families rarely receive).

As is clear from the practice of the Eastern Church, there is no incompatibility between the sacrament of matrimony and the sacrament of holy orders. In the Eastern churches religious order priests practice celibacy, parish priests are married. Ironically, in the West the opposite approach might make more sense. The religious orders teach high schools and colleges, which one can do just about as well married or single; it is precisely the parish clergy who ought to be free for the vigorous demands of parochial life in the United States.

It would be naive to expect a change in the practice of celibacy in the immediate future, however sympathetic the laity might be to such a change. The hierarchies of the world at the present time seem almost certainly to be overwhelmingly against it. Part of the problem, in my mind, at any rate, is that once marriage becomes an option it almost becomes an obligation, as both our Eastern and Anglican brothers and sisters have experienced. The unmarried clergyman in a situation of optional celibacy is even more of a threat, and far more likely to be suspected of homosexuality.

In the present state of human sexual attitudes, it might be very difficult to preserve celibacy as a valid option. Certainly a change should not occur until some method is found for preserving the celibate option and not de facto eliminate it from Catholic life.

RECOMMENDATIONS TO PRESENT
AND FUTURE PARISH PRIESTS

1) THERE are few objective grounds either in the theological or the social sciences for the identity crisis which presently torments you. We do not deny the reality of either the crisis or the torment and do not seek to minimize the difficulties under which local religious leadership must currently labor. Our point, rather, is that there are resources available to transcend the present questions of identity. You may very well feel cheated by the fact that neither your theologians nor your episcopal leaders have yet provided you with these resources. In fact, for the time being, you may have to dig them out yourself. Nonetheless you are not without enormous resources and in time these resources will lead to the dawn of a new era of local community religious leadership.

2) The rise of the lay ministries—however they may be defined—does not make the priest less important. On the contrary, the new ministries increase the demand for the coordinating-through-comfort-and-challenge style of leadership which is at the core of the priestly role.

3) The Sunday homily is one of the most important things you do. You must prepare for it both directly in the efforts that go into it each week and indirectly by developing your creative imagination so that you are skilled at telling the stories of God and the stories of Faith which are the essence of Catholic Christianity. The priest who preaches a good homily will be forgiven many other leadership faults.

4) The precinct captain model recommended in this book has skills essential for the work of comforting and challenging. No one can be expected to be born with such skills. They are acquired

through practice and mistakes—and never by the faint hearted or the cautious. To grow at these skills requires constant supportive feedback from your colleagues and your people. You must build such feedback into your life.

5) You must value the American form of local religious community which, as we have said, is absolutely unique in all the world. All too frequently in the last three decades we Americans have looked to other models—the city parishes of Paris, the worker priests of Mission France, the *Communitas de basso* of Latin America—as though they were the answers to American problems. While it is doubtless the case that we can learn much from the local communities of every corner of the Catholic world (and they from us, as far as that goes), we have often envied other nations their "new" religious forms without giving so much as the slightest thought that there is something positive to be said about the neighborhood/parish which grew up in the ethnic immigrant experience in this country. Yet, in fact, it is a highly successful innovation in church structure. It ought to be understood and valued in its own right. More to the point, perhaps, it is where we are. Even if one does not wish to celebrate the neighborhood parish one must at least concede that it is what we have. You will not go beyond it unless you understand it and value what is good about it. This will require that you leave aside, at least for the moment, any attempt to graft foreign growths on it and study both the theology and the social science of the American local religious community.

6) You must therefore require from your own leadership both a much more highly developed theory—based on the theological and human disciplines—of the American parish and the kind of in-service training which will help you to develop the skills of comfort and challenge which are required as you play your question-asking, precinct captain-listening, story telling role.

Chapter Three

———

The Church Has a "Woman Problem"

LISTEN, GUYS, IT'S SERIOUS!

GIVEN the social and educational changes among the American Catholic laity and given the large number of Catholic women with occupations and careers before the Second Vatican Council, it does not seem likely that the changes in the church instituted by the council can account for the rise of Catholic "feminism" and for the anger among many American Catholic women at what they perceive as the church's commitment to traditional rigid gender-linked role definitions.

Some religious leaders console themselves with the image of the traditional Catholic wife and mother: strong but obedient, vigorous but docile, dedicated, loyal, devout, transmitting to her children the traditional Catholic religious truths that have been passed on by women like her for centuries, women like their mothers and their sisters, such leaders would like to believe. This is the way, such leaders tell themselves, most Catholic women still are. It is only a handful of nuns or lesbians or radicals who want to be ordained or who want equal power in the church with men.

One suspects that if priests and bishops think that way they have not seriously discussed the issue with their sisters or their mothers. American Catholic women and men have rejected at least in principle and in theory and have rejected by overwhelming majorities the traditional gender role definitions. It may not be at all clear to them what this rejection is going to mean for the future either in their personal or their religious life, but the equality of man and woman in theory and principle at any rate is supported by most Catholic men and women—and Catholics were more likely to support the late Equal Rights Amendment than the national average.

The "woman problem" then, seems to be not so much the result of the Second Vatican Council, as something that happened after the council, another case of the convergence of religious change with trends of social and economic change which were already at work and which would have had a considerable impact on American Catholicism if it had not been for the council. It may well be that the greater toleration of the parish clergy for such changes, a toleration based on their interpretation of the council's spirit if not the council's letter, has made the "woman problem" less serious for the church rather than more serious. Indeed, it may be that the greater tolerance of the parish clergy for the changing behavior and value patterns of American Catholics has eased many of the acute problems which would have occurred in any case because of the changing social and economic condition of American Catholics.

One has the impression that the leadership of the American hierarchy is now only too well aware that it has a "woman problem" and indeed is juggling its proposed pastoral on women as it would the most sizzling of hot potatoes. One also has the impression that the leadership of the American Church has not prevailed upon the Vatican to believe that the "woman problem" is as serious as they, the American bishops, perceive it to be—either because they have not argued the case vigorously enough or (as may be more likely) the Vatican hasn't wished to listen carefully enough.

In any event, the point must be made as forcefully as possible: The "woman problem" is serious, very serious indeed. And one cannot imagine a way in which it is not going to get even more serious in the years ahead.

A QUESTION OF MISSED OPPORTUNITIES

JOHN XXIII endorsed feminism in one of his social encyclicals, but this has not changed the thinking of large numbers of church-persons on the role of women. Nor has it led the Church in practice to turn the governance of women religious over to women. The history of Christianity has been marked by considerable ambivalence on the subject of women. Certainly in the early Church women seem to have had far more freedom and power than they did in pagan institutions. In the Middle Ages women presided over monasteries, ruled counties, assigned parish priests, gave confessional jurisdiction, and probably had more power in general than they had in any era before or since. It is also true that women religious in the United States have more check-signing power than women do in any other corporate institution. On the other hand, nuns have often been treated like second-class citizens, have been dominated by priests (and often inept priests at that), and have been excluded from policy-making roles in the Church. The Church's history, in other words, on the subject of women is complex. We have much to be ashamed of in our treatment of women; we also have a record that is better than that of most human institutions. The position on the ordination of women is allegedly based on the symbolism of the Eucharist, but the argument does not seem inherently persuasive. If anything, the Eucharist as a sacrament of nourishment might as well be maternal as paternal. Until the Holy Office statement on the ordination of women, only somewhat less than one-third of American Catholics supported it. But in the months immediately after the statement was issued, support moved up to almost one-half. One of the reasons for Roman opposition to ordination of women is fear of offending the Orthodox churches; Rome, oddly enough, is much more afraid of offending the Orthodox than it is of offending the Anglicans. Women will eventually be ordained in the Catholic Church, I suspect, but it may take

69

several more decades. In the meantime the Church continues to miss many opportunities to provide illumination and direction for those women who value marriage, family, and motherhood yet do not want their life energies to be completely directed to gender-linked roles. Some people articulate a reactionary and patronizing approach to women, others preach militant feminism, which in its own way is equally as patronizing. For the vast middle majority the Church does not have much to say. In some sense the ordination of women controversy has distracted the Church from this broader question. To put the matter in proper perspective, as is mentioned elsewhere in this book, the average woman at one time needed ten pregnancies to reproduce herself and would very likely be dead before her childbearing years were over. (Lucrezia Borgia died at 39, giving birth to her seventh child, which was stillborn—the fourth of her children not to survive.) Today many women can have accomplished the reproduction necessary to continue the race before they are 25, with their children safely in school before they are 30. The Church simply does not seem able to grasp the importance of this profound demographic change.

WHY CAN'T WOMEN BECOME PRIESTS?

I SIMPLY do not believe the arguments against women priests; but the arguments that one hears are as follows:
Jesus was a man. Jesus didn't choose any women to be his apostles. The church has never had women priests. The symbolism of the Eucharist requires that a man preside over it.

Candidly, I think these are rotten arguments. Jesus did not ordain priests in the sense that we ordain them. He merely gathered followers and entrusted them with a mission of organizing his community. In the Palestinian Judaism of his time, the culture was sufficiently patriarchal that the question of women presiding over the Eucharist simply did not and could not occur (though the attitude of Jesus towards women, his respect and affection for them, the fairness of his treatment of them were so remarkable that by themselves they might constitute a powerful argument that Jesus was no mere human being). It is not clear that women have not presided over the Eucharistic assembly at various times in Christian history. Indeed, there are some traces of evidence available that suggest they have on occasion been Eucharistic presidents and even perhaps bishops. Obvious and sometimes crude attempts have been made to cover up these historical phenomena. The argument about male symbolism in the Eucharist is a mish-mash of nonsense, as are most arguments based on symbols that are made by theologians and church leaders who do not understand what a complex, dense, multi-layered and polyvalent thing a symbol is.

My own feeling is that opposition to women priests comes from the profound male chauvinism of many church leaders born of the fear that any changes, particularly such a drastic change, will be an enormous threat to the power of the Roman curia. Indeed, it is a good rule of thumb that when anyone advances problematic theological and symbolic reasons to oppose a change, the real issue isn't theology at all but organizational power. Finally, many if

71

not most men fear women. Priests and bishops are no different from any others. Indeed, some church leaders are clearly sexually neutered, do not like women, do not find them attractive, try to avoid them whenever possible, and would find their whole being threatened if they had to share the ministry with women.

On the other hand, I'm not altogether sure that women in the priesthood will improve the church any more than the women's vote improved politics. It is a change which I think right and just, but not one which finally is going to make all that much difference in what the church is.

ANGRY CATHOLIC WOMEN

THE modestly popular play *Sister Mary Ignatius Explains It All* is a devastating attack by a very angry playwright on the Catholic education and the Catholic church of his childhood. Sister Mary Ignatius is an arrogant, rigid, narrow, oppressive manifestation of counter reformation Catholics. No one familiar with the Church of a quarter century ago will deny the reality of such persons, even if they were not the only kind of parochial school teachers in that era.

But one wonders why the fury at her and what she stood for, a fury which can be found in many other alienated Catholic writers. That form of Catholicism is as dead as Arianism. By now Sister Mary Ignatius is either married to a priest or marching on a picket line. She is as rigid as she ever was, but Catholics have no monopoly on rigidity.

Yet the angry writers and the other angry Catholics of that generation will not be put off by such a response. They don't care what Catholicism is today. They are still angry at what it was and the relationship between what it was and the problems in their lives. Indeed, they do not want to hear the Church has changed, because a change will have deprived them of a convenient scapegoat.

To say that the Church is a scapegoat for their anger is not to justify the Catholicism of Sister Mary Ignatius or to criticize the anger of those who still hate her and what she stood for. But not everyone who sat in classrooms presided over by such nuns is angry at the Church. The issue then becomes why some Catholics focus on one aspect of the Catholic tradition and others on another aspect. The image of Sister Mary Ignatius represents an intensely unpleasant experience in the playwright's childhood and the image lingers, affecting even today his image of Church. His experience of her has become a symbol which is an important part of his life story.

Perhaps the story can be changed—our data suggest it might be by a devout and progressive and loving Catholic spouse—but it will not be changed easily.

Religious images, in this theory, are preconscious—not repressed but not attended to either. They become patterns, paradigms, templates for response to life and to religion as well as symbols of past experiences. The phenomenon which we have investigated in this monograph is but one of a whole species of religious reactions in which an institution is judged by a past experience, an experience which is intense, frustrating and infuriating but which was not the only possible experience even in the past.

Yet to those who suffered the experience, it seems to have been the only possible one until some new and powerful experience deletes it. Those who are bitterly angry at the Sister Mary Ignatius's of their past simply cannot believe that all Catholics do not share such an experience. Those "feminist" women who are "turned off" by the Church are doubtless astonished and sceptical when they encounter other "feminist" women whose experiences do not preclude high levels of religious devotion.

The key, of course, is the family. I had a couple of teachers not unlike Sister Mary Ignatius in school and laughed them off because my family experience was benign for the most part and what was not benign was not identified with the Church. Moreover, whatever conflicts I've had in adult life have not come from ambivalent family experiences which are linked in my imagination with Church.

As a psychiatrist once remarked, "I know a priest has begun to mature when he stops blaming his problems on the seminary and begins to examine his family experiences."

Again, these comments are made not to excuse the Church of the past or the Church of the present for the attitudes towards women, which I find deplorable and intolerable. Rather, they are an attempt at an explanation of why these attitudes drive some "feminist" women away from the Church and do not drive others away.

Briefly, there are four persons who seem to suppress the negative correlation between "feminism" and church attendance—Mother, Spouse, Priest and God. The Mother must be non-traditional either in her church attendance or her occupational career. The Spouse must be devout and it helps if he is also a "feminist." And God must be seen as a "Lover," which She/He is likely to become .if the Spouse and the Mother are appropriate "sacraments."

The point in these observations is that negative images and image incompatibilities are deep and complex but not utterly immut able. The family past probably cannot be changed or even reexamined, short of intense therapy. The spouse is at least a new influence and a new image which is of enormous importance. Do you want to bring a "feminist" young woman back to Church? Well, find her a devout, loving, and "feminist" spouse. There is a chance that she is already looking for one anyway.

And if God does not change, surely the image the Church presents of Him/Her can change (change back, I would suggest). In part, perhaps the personalities of Church leaders can help effect such a change. Pope John surely had such an impact, as did John Paul I, the smiling September Pope (who, in keeping with a little known but powerful church tradition, talked of God as a Mother). So did John Paul II until his image took on a tone of nay saying and repression (an image I happen to think is inaccurate but which is almost universal, especially among those who have a negative image of Church to begin with).

However, "let's get to know one another" sessions in the parish or the election of women to parish councils or the appointment of women to diocesan "cabinets"—however meritorious such actions and activities may be—will simply not touch the image incompatibilities which this research has unearthed.

If church leaders are interested in actually "evangelizing" alienated Catholic women, instead of merely talking about it, then they must resign themselves to the fact that they have an enormous problem on their hands, a problem rooted in the mistakes of the past indeed but confirmed by continuing mistakes in the present.

And probably the first change ought to be in their own personalities and attitudes.

Alas, clergy (of all faiths) are much better at telling others to change than at changing themselves.

STORM WARNINGS

IN THE summer of 1983 two incidents occurred which neatly il-
lustrated the problems involved in any attempt by the Catholic
Church to respond to its alienated women members—the dismissal
from the religious life of Sister Mary Mancour by the Archbishop
of Detroit and the ban on women servers at Mass by the Cardinal
Archbishop of Chicago.

In a Church in which the leadership was aware of the magnitude
of the problem of women's alienation neither crisis would have
been permitted to happen. The Archbishop of Detroit felt free to
force a nun out of the religious life to reassert his power and
authority and the Cardinal Archbishop of Chicago was astonished
by the vehemence of the reaction of his routine letter on "altar
girls" because church leadership is monumentally insensitive to
the dimensions of its "women problem."

One member of the chancery staff in Chicago told a woman on
a committee protesting the altar girl ban that the majority of Catholic women in Chicago did not agree with her. It is to be wondered
how he knew. Surely there is no empirical evidence to support
his argument nor is there any inclination to seek the empirical
evidence. The non-existence of a women problem is not an empirical conclusion but an *a priori* act of faith with much of the
clergy and most of the hierarchy. As a matter of definition, "feminism" is limited only to a few nuns who want to be ordained and
a few outspoken supporters of ERA and/or abortion. The good
Catholic wife and mother of myth and fable is presumed to be
as loyal as she always was to ecclesiastical authority.

Such a mentality precludes the possibility of church authority
responding to the problem we have outlined in this report. And
the Detroit and Chicago scandals of the summer of '83 reveal how
simple-minded the mentality is.

Probably neither case caused many women to discontinue church attendance. As we have explained in this book, it is past history rather than present reality which accounts for "anger" (as we have defined it). Doubtless the Mancour case and the altar girl ban have made a lot of Catholic women angry in the ordinary sense of that word. But as we have also tried to explain that anger does not turn people away from the Church; it rather makes them even more furious participants.

It is not that church authorities do not care about the anger, in either sense of the word; rather, they simply do not see it because they refuse to admit its possibility. The data in the present report must be rejected out of hand because it does not fit the unassailable paradigms of the ecclesiastical mind.

Hence there is no need to take seriously the positive pastoral suggestions presented in the constructive part of our study. The typical bishop and the typical pastor might agree that the recommendations are interesting and indeed would be very useful if the Church had a massive "women problem." But since it does not, then the recommendations can safely be ignored. It is a fairly melancholy conclusion, but one which at the present time is inescapable. Church leadership does not see a women problem because it does not want to, perhaps because it is afraid to.

It is the response of men on a low lying coast with storm warnings posted for all to see and the eye of the hurricane rushing towards them, who still insist that it is not even raining.

Chapter Four

**Is Catholic Sexual Teaching
Coming Apart?**

IS CATHOLIC SEXUAL
TEACHING COMING APART?

THE encyclical *Humanae Vitae* was for all practical purposes an appeal to pure authority, a pure authority which the Pope mistakenly assumed that he still had. The Pope did list the arguments in favor of contraception, but he did not even bother to propound an intellectual response to them; he, in effect, dismissed them, and reasserted the prohibition against birth control couched entirely in terms of its being a prohibition based on "God's law." It is precisely here that the differences between the Pope and the majority of priests and laity seems to exist. Many people simply do not believe any longer that such a prohibition is part of the divine law, and they do not believe the Pope in terms of pure authority can say that it is.

The question immediately arises—and it did on the floor of the Bishops' meeting when we made our presentation of the basic findings of the research project—that if priests still believe in God and the Church, how can they reconcile their faith with a rejection of papal authority on a matter so important? By the logic of the old formulation, such a rejection may indeed be inconsistent; but the point is that the logic of the old formulations is no longer accepted. Those priests and laity who reject the birth control teaching simply refuse to believe that they are rejecting something that is of the essence of either Christianity or Catholicism. In effect, what they are rejecting is the papal claim to be the uniquely authentic interpreter of Christianity on the point of birth control. They are not, on their own terms at least, rejecting Christianity, but they are rejecting a misunderstanding or misinterpretation of it. The Pope, in other words, has made a serious, indeed tragic, mistake and they are not going to be bound by his mistakes.

It is not my purpose to repeat the arguments in favor of a change in the birth control position. It is clear that the fundamental

81

weakness of the official stance is that it has proved incapable of taking into account either the massive world population problem or the development of sexual pesonalism that has occurred in the wake of the dramatic new insights of depth psychology. The official teaching is still caught in a mentality of population shortage, in the physical mechanics of procreation instead of the psychic dynamics of human love, in the authoritarian structure of the peasant family instead of the democratic structure of the modern urban family. The world of the official birth control position is one of the eighteenth century. While fundamental morality does not change with the centuries, the human context of moral behavior does. The fundamental theme of Catholic sexual morality is a respect for life; it is an important theme, desperately needed in the modern world, but it has been caught in certain rigid formulations, which not only obscure its basic content but seem to outsiders to represent the opposite of a concern for life. The negative prohibitions of the official sexual morality could be maintained only by the overwhelming force of a rigid, static, authoritarian Church. As soon as the post-Tridentine ecclesiastical organization began to collapse, the credibility of the official sexual teaching evanesced, and Catholic moralists were completely unprepared to provide either a new rationale for the old ethic or a new line of development by which the old ethic could grow and transform itself. If Paul VI relied on sheer, naked authority in *Humanae Vitae,* only part of the explanation is that he unwisely thought he still possessed such authority. The rest of the explanation is that there was nothing else for him to do. He was unable to advance any solid arguments against change (and indeed against the majority of his own birth control commission) because he didn't have any such arguments. And neither did anyone else....

Humanae Vitae is a misfortune not because priests and laity take it seriously. The image of the obedient Catholic laity bravely shouldering an almost impossible burden is simply invalid (no matter how much the Pope and his advisors or his most extreme critics inside and outside the Church would have it so). Rather, *Humanae Vitae* was a tragedy because it destroyed for many Catholics and for many priests their confidence in ecclesiastical leadership, and brought to a definitive end the optimism and euphoria which the Vatican Council had engendered. *Humanae Vitae* is a symbol of the whole Pauline papacy: With all possible good intentions, Paul VI tried to slow down the pace of change so that the transition from the old to the new would be orderly, but he completely misread the strength and the direction of the forces the Vatican Council unleashed in the Church. Instead of creating orderly change, Paul VI turned a highly fluid, dynamic, and complicated situation into chaos—and it will be a long time before the pieces will be put back together again.

It is likely to be a very long time before the Church recaptures any kind of credibility as a teacher of sexual morality. Indeed, it must be said in all honesty that as long as the shadow of the *Humanae Vitae* prohibition hangs over the Church, there is not the slightest likelihood of any progress towards the re-establishment of credibility. The Catholic family movements (Cana and CFM, for example) are in sad disarray. Based in part on a theory of large families, Cana and CFM were moving in the 60s in the direction of some kind of Christian personalism (though in many instances, it was a rather shallow variety). *Humanae Vitae* brought an end to all of that, not so much because the members felt the need to throw away their contraceptives, but because of the smashing blow of the Pope's refusal to even seriously consider the question. In a Church where the papal figure is not as important as he has been for the last several hundred years, theoreticians would not have been so staggered by a papal encyclical. But in the Church of the 1960s, the papal authority figure still loomed in gigantic proportion. The obstacles to the development of new theories are not legal but psychological. When the official Church appears to have closed its mind on the possibility of development of sexual teaching and remains rigidly fixated in the eighteenth century, the reaction of most theoreticians is to throw up their hands in despair and say, in effect, "Why bother to try?"

The result may very well be a period of pure permissiveness in which, for want of anything better to say, priests will tell lay people that the Church is incapable of providing any kind of guidance in the sexual field, and that it is pretty much all right to do whatever they want. Our data do not show that such a phenomenon has occurred as yet; most priests still reject premarital sex, although young priests are somewhat more likely to approve of it than older priests.

But the important point is that there is no great demand for legitimation of premarital sex. Despite all the articles in the popular press to the contrary, there is no evidence that chastity is any less prevalent now than it was in the past—which is not to say that it ever has been all that prevalent. The overwhelming majority of Americans still believe, in theory if not in practice, in premarital chastity—probably as much as they did in the past and probably as much as they are going to in the future. Despite the widely publicized cohabitation among college students (one would think that they are the first group of young human beings in history to take lovers), the social norm against extramarital sex still stands, and hence the Catholic position is supported by the wider social position—a situation which is exactly opposite from the birth control question. In other words, at the present time the Roman Catholic Church has nothing persuasive or effective to add to general social norms of sexual morality. In the midst of Western man's frantic efforts to assimilate the wisdom of depth psychology and philosophical personalism, the only contribution the Catholic Church apparently is capable of making seems limited to a handwringing concern about the physical mechanics of procreation. Surely we could do better.

What is needed is a whole new theory of sexual morality, probably one less concerned with specific negative prohibitions and more concerned with the fascinating religious symbolism of human love as an image of the relationship between Christ and his Church and vice versa. Surely a Church which has an intercourse symbol of the lighted candle being plunged into water at the center of the Easter liturgy must have some wisdom to contribute to the human quest for a deeper understanding of the great mysteries of sexuality and love. It would not be fair to say that there is nothing being done by the psychologists, theologians, philosophers, and theoreticians, toward developing a Christian vision of sexuality, but it would not be an exaggeration to say that very little is being done, and that little is likely to be done as long as the Church is bogged down in the swamps of *Humanae Vitae*. Most Catholics will continue to live lives of relative chastity under the influence of the general sexual norms of the society. Young Catholics will go through the sexual maturation process with no more wisdom available to them than is available to any of their fellow Americans. Bizarre aberrations, such as the nude marathon encounter, will have as much if not more appeal to the sexually confused Catholics as to their sexually confused fellow Americans. (One hears that at Esalen nuns are among the most enthusiastic frequenters of the nude marathon.) And the clergy, entrusted *ex officio* with the solemn responsibility of interpreting the implications of the message of Jesus for human life will have to shrug their shoulders and say that as far as they know, there are no special implications of the Good News for human sexuality. Bishops, aware that many of their priests will no longer attempt to impose the official position (though probably refusing to believe how extensive that refusal is) will awkwardly look the other way, knowing that the official position went out of fashion long ago and that they have no real power to impose the papal decision on their priests.

Some Recommendations

At this point the encyclical *Humanae Vitae* is a dead letter, and there is no point in attempting to revoke it. What is needed, rather,

85

is the beginning of a new approach in which the Holy See urges Catholic scholars and practitioners to begin to re-examine the Christian tradition and reformulate the sexual wisdom of that tradition in terms that provide assistance to modern man. It should encourage attempts to determine which methods of family planning are acceptable and which are unacceptable. This will almost certainly exceed the competence of Church authority.

The Church must ask itself, given the present situation—in which the traditional teaching as embodied by *Humanae Vitae* enjoys no credibility at all—where ought we to begin anew in our attempt to provide meaning and interpretation for human sexuality? Such new attempts obviously imply a *de facto* acceptance of the reality of the failure of *Humanae Vitae,* but recognizing that truth is far less important, it seems to me, than trying to begin again somewhere else.

It is probably essential to acknowledge that mistakes have been made. Indeed, I see no way for the Church to begin to re-establish credibility in the sexual area without acknowledging the horrendous mistakes of the past. I am not a theologian, and I do not propose to try to explain how such mistakes can be harmonized with the Church's claim to infallibility, though heaven knows vast numbers of other mistakes have been made in the past. The fundamental concern, of course, for the sanctity of human life is not a mistake, but that concern has manifested itself in ways that clearly have been mistaken. A view of ecclesiastical authority which refuses to admit the possibility of mistakes in formulation is precisely that view which has got us into the present mess; it must be abandoned before we can extricate ourselves from it. We can expect no progress during the present papacy.

The position of most priests is an extremely awkward one. They can, of course, give private advice in the confessional or in counseling sessions that is at variance with the official and public teaching of the Church. But they must be wary of how open they are with such advice. A peculiar, implicit gentleman's agreement has developed between clergy and hierarchy in which the hierarchy commits itself not to try seriously to enforce compliance with *Humanae Vitae* so long as the clergy is not too open and public in its opposition to the encyclical. Such an agreement may be necessary in the present organizational context of the Church, but it is a sad judgment on that organizational context that such devious, not to say dishonest, procedures have to be followed. I can think of no practical recommendation that can be made on the subject. Obviously, the long range solution is to change the organizational context so that those whose cooperation is necessary for the implementation of any ecclesiastical decision will be deeply involved in making the decisions—a principle of the human relations approach to organization which ought to be obvious even without the theology of collegiality.

But the ordinary priest can do little without leadership, scholarship, theory, or even the promise of the beginnings of theory. Men and women being what they are, they will almost certainly continue to turn to their religious leaders for advice on their sexual problems, and the Catholic clergy are in a singularly bad position to give such advice. Their only consolation is that the human race has an excellent record for not taking seriously the advice of its religious leaders on a wide variety of subjects, most especially sexuality.

MORALITY

PROPERLY speaking, the Catholic Church is not in the morality business at all despite the impression most of us got when we were growing up. The Church is in the religion business, and religion and morality—again despite our impressions—are not the same thing. Both are practical theories, not speculative like philosophy; both deal with how one lives. But religion explains the ultimate purposes of human life and of the existence of the cosmos of which we are a part.

Religion tells us whether it's safe to hope, to trust, to take chances, to seriously accept the primal thrust of the human personality toward the conviction that life does have a purpose that transcends itself and that it is safe to love.

Morality is a system of principles covering the day-to-day choices between good and evil humankind must make. Religion tells us that the world and its processes are ultimately good (or perhaps evil); morality tells us what kind of human behavior is good. The two are obviously related, because one's decisions about the nature of the universe and the purposes of human life create the context in which moral choices must be made; but many people with different visions of the ultimate purpose of human life can still agree on fundamental moral principles, because the consequences of human behavior are the same no matter what one's ultimate worldview.

Neither Jesus nor St. Paul were systematic ethicians; they were rather prophets (in Jesus' case, of course, more than prophet), teachers of religion, expounders of a worldview, men who claimed to have a vision of who God was and why he created us. Both, indeed, vigorously resisted the hyperlegalization of the Jewish ethical theory in the environment in which they lived. Neither hesitated to offer moral advice to his followers, but moral concerns were secondary to religious ones. Christian thinkers after the time

88

of Jesus and St. Paul and the other apostles developed a specific moral heritage in which the traditional wisdom of the Greek, Roman, and Hebrew moral thinkers was reformulated to some considerable extent in light of the Christian insights about the meaning of the world and the meaning of human life. This Christian morality was derived from twin sources, the gospel and the philosophical systems of the early eras and then subsequent eras.

Obviously the Christian moral theory must be taken very seriously by those who claim to be followers of Jesus of Nazareth because it is the only one that claims to be illumined by the revelation of the nature of God that was contained in the life, death, and resurrection of Jesus. (Of course, within the Christian moral system there are many different traditions.) Most of this book is concerned with moral questions rather than religious questions in the strict sense of the word. Moral questions are important; they are less important than religious questions. They are also easier to answer and easier to live by. It is much easier to keep the law than to respond enthusiastically and generously to the passionate love of God which was revealed in Jesus. Unfortunately for the legalist in all of us, Jesus made it very clear that it was passionate love he required, not merely moral obedience.

PREMARITAL SEX

IN discussing this subject one must carefully separate the issue of physical virginity from the issue of sexual love. A strong emphasis on physical virginity is not part of the Catholic Chrisitan heritage; it is a cultural component which attached itself to Catholicism in the ancient world because of the contention that the virginity of a wife was essential to guarantee that one's land and property were truly passed on to one's own seed, to members of one's own tribe. The bride price paid at the time of marriage to the father of the bride was a purchased guarantee of the inviolate hymen of his daughter, a guarantee which was economically important. The cultural norm that has led to an obsession with physical virginity has survived long after it ceased to be economically relevant. The Church has mistakenly permitted its teaching to be infected by this archaic and indeed inhuman attitude.

If Catholics abstain from premarital sex, the reasons have nothing to do with physical virginity and a lot to do with the nature of the Catholic conviction about human love. We believe that human love reflects the single-minded, passionate, total commitment of God to his people, of Christ to his Church; and we are convinced that the central love is only authentically Christian within the context of such commitment. Our chastity is not physical but "mysterious" or eschatological in the sense of revealing, making real, manifesting, demonstrating a higher love which dominates the universe. The ultimate reason why young Catholics should be urged to practice chastity is that followers of Jesus of Nazareth, young people who are committed to reflecting the presence of God in the world, do so by saving their sexual love until it can adequately reflect a single-minded, permanent, passionate commitment. It may be argued that this approach will not convince very many people who do not want to be convinced. So be it; and so much for our failures to explain to young people what Christianity is all about. It might be noted, however, that the argument proposed here is the only one that is truly effective against the attitude, "Well, I've lost my virginity, so now what the hell difference does it make?"

It should also be noted that there is no psychological evidence at all that premarital promiscuity, living together, or any other such arrangements have any effect on the later adjustment of marriage. Indeed, the sexual permissiveness on the college campuses at the present time is frequently just a new form of male exploitation masquerading as ideological liberalism. Chastity may not be a better preparation for marriage, but it is certainly not worse than promiscuity.

Within this framework the question still remains as to whether if marriage is indeed a process (see *Annulment*), need sexual intimacy wait until the formalities of a wedding—especially when a couple is clearly and decisively committed to one another? I'll pass on this one and leave it to moral theologians braver than I to assay an answer. I must say, however, that the moral positions we learned in the seminary, which limited healthy engaged young men and women to quick kisses and gentle hand holding, seems in retrospect to have been extraordinarily naive and quite possibly psychologically damaging, because it assumed that people could leap from a relationship in which there was no expressed passion to one in which passion was totally expressed within the space of twenty-four hours. Most young people knew better and acted according-ly—with guilty consciences, perhaps, but not feeling they were doing anything "terribly wrong." I do not know where this leaves us on the subject of that favorite teenage sin of yesteryear, "necking and petting," and I defer to the moral theologians and psychologists on the subject. I would simply submit that the Church would be much better advised to use its resources to train its young people in the skills of generosity, patience, and self-sacrifice required for sustained human intimacy instead of harassing them about fondling and passionate kissing. Indeed, one might go so far as to

91

say that the Church would be well advised to seek ways to assure that its young people are capable of maintaining a high level of sexual playfulness after marriage instead of preventing this playfulness before marriage.

Having said all these things, I must add that it is my conviction both as a priest and as a social scientist that religiously, psychologically, and humanly, chastity is far superior to promiscuity, and that in the sexual act there is a built-in strain toward permanence which ought to be taken far more seriously than it is today.

ABORTION

CATHOLIC teaching insists that the foetus is a human person and has all the right of a human person. Hence the termination of the life of a foetus is murder. There is relatively little difference between Protestants and Catholics in America on the question of legalization of abortion. The majority of both religious groups support it under certain circumstances (risk of the life of the mother) and oppose it under other circumstances (a woman simply does not want to have a child). But it is important to note that while Catholics are tolerant of the civil legalization of abortion, they do so as good pluralists, unwilling to impose their own moral beliefs on others. Over 90 percent of American Catholics say that they themselves would not seek an abortion or would not want their spouse to seek one.

Yet the Catholic prohibition against terminating the life of a child is not absolute. Under some circumstances, for example, ectopic pregnancies or a severely diseased uterus, according to Catholic moral theory, operations are licit which de facto will lead to the death of the child. Such termination of pregnancies is justified in light of the moral "principle of double effect": an operation with two results, one good and one bad, with the bad result not flowing from the good one. Of course, once one has conceded the possibility that there are certain kinds of "Catholic abortion," one has acknowledged that the issue is a good deal more complicated than simply a foetus's right to life. There are few if any Catholic theologians who are ready to defend abortion, though some Catholic women activists (not excluding nuns) have campaigned for a woman's right to make her own decision about abortion on the grounds that every woman has a right to make a decision over her own body, as though control over one's body were absolute. (Nobody, as far as I know, would argue that our control over our own bodies is such that we can ingest large amounts of alcohol

93

into the bloodstream and then drive an automobile through a crowd of people on the grounds that we can do whatever we want with our bodies.) However, some Catholics have wondered when human life is present in the foetus. They are not completely persuaded that a single fertilized ovum is indeed a human person. The Scholastics in the Middle Ages were not persuaded either, though for reasons that are today perceived as biologically erroneous. The biological and philosophical issues affecting the question of when human life begins in the womb are complicated and perhaps insoluble. Supporters of abortion argue that a human person is present only when a baby is capable of existing outside its mother's womb. (Though some abortion supporters also argue that infanticide is no different from abortion and is a logical consequence of it. They are a small minority, however.)

There are few questions in American society which are more vigorously controverted than the abortion issue. Dialogue between the two sides seems to be extremely difficult. Many Catholics, the present writer included, cannot understand how men and women of good faith and good will do not perceive that a three-months old embryo is indeed human and must be respected as human. It must be said honestly, however, that many abortion supporters are men and women of sincerity, honesty, and good faith. In a civilized society we ought to strive to understand the logic and rationale of their position even if we cannot accept it; and they must strive to understand our position too. But these preliminary dialogues seem quite impossible in the highly emotional atmosphere of the current abortion debate.

Catholics should also realize that while their position is currently described as "unliberal," there was a time, when the anti-abortion laws were written (mostly under Protestant auspices, be it noted), that such protection of the life of the unborn was considered to be a notable and progressive advance for civilization. Abortion and infanticide are the two principal means of population control that the human race has used down through its history. Even as recently as the last part of the nineteenth century, tens of thousands of neonates or foetuses were destroyed every year by exposure, by drowning, by being put out to baby farms. The waters of the Thames and the Seine carried them off by the scores every night of the year. All the churches vigorously opposed abortion and infanticide during the worst of the nineteenth-century epidemic brought on by the population explosion of that time. Catholicism remains true to that liberal and civilized theme; but it does so against the age-old practices of humankind and against the de facto practices of many of its own people in past years. All species practice forms of population control when disease and violent death fail to keep the population within psychologically tolerable limits. The killing of foetuses and babies, appalling as it may seem to contemporary Catholics, has been the response of humankind to population pressures throughout its history, a response which apparently troubled very few consciences. These facts are noted not to defend abortion, not to suggest that Catholics abandon their opposition to it; but simply so that the issue may be seen in the proper historical perspective.

WHY CAN'T CATHOLICS
PRACTICE BIRTH CONTROL?

WELL, in fact most of them do, not only in the United States but in most of the other Catholic countries of the North Atlantic world, and they practice birth control because they are convinced that the Pope is simply wrong on this issue and that he and other church leaders do not appreciate how important sex is for keeping married love alive. Those who study the nature of human nature in the physical and biological sciences would agree that sex as a pair-bonding mechanism is more important in humans than it is in the rest of the primate species. Relatively frequent marital sex seems to be an essential part of human nature and when the church seems to want to inhibit and perhaps even prohibit this relationship, it is in the awkward position of seeming to violate one aspect of the natural law in the name of supporting another aspect.

Basically, the argument of the birth control encyclical is twofold:

a) The natural law is violated when some "artificial" impediment is used to prevent each and every act of marital intercourse from being open to the possibility of conception.

b) The sacramental symbolism of married love is violated when an impediment of an artificial nature is permitted to interfere with fertility.

This is the official, though non-infallible, teaching of the church. Many Catholic theologians and priests believe that the teaching can be reconsidered, especially because both the arguments seem dubious. Everything we know from the natural sciences about human nature suggests that that which is specifically human about the sexuality of our primate species is oriented towards pair-bonding and as long as the act of sexual intercourse is open to the possibility of pair-bonding it does not violate the essence of human nature. The overwhelming majority of Pope John's Birth Control Commission agreed with this position and argued that a marriage considered as a whole had to be open to the possibility of conception, but not necessarily each marriage act. Moreover, it is the almost unanimous experience of married couples that contraceptive intercourse does not interfere with the full expression of married love and does not lead to deterioration of respect for woman as church teachers insist that it does.

This controversy is one of the most serious that Catholicism has ever faced, both because of the great importance of sex in the lives of married people and because of the fundamental and pervasive dissent from the official teaching on the part not only of the married laity but also on the part of the lower clergy.

The root of the problem, it seems to me, is the absence of institutions of communication by which the laity can inform leadership of the church of the experience and wisdom of their married lives. The Pope, in his exhortation, *Familiaris Consortio*, has insisted that the married lay people have a unique and indispensible contribution to make to our church's understanding of marital morality by virtue of the charism of the sacrament of holy matrimony. Unfortunately, the birth control discussion has gone on now for fifty years with no attempt made to give the laity a chance to speak to the church leadership about their experience of married love, and in particular about their experience that the church's attitude on birth control creates an enormous impediment to the expression of married love. We have, it is to be feared, replaced the irreplaceable and dispensed with the indispensable. Until institutions of communication are established whereby the church leadership can listen to the authentic voice of the laity (and not merely to the voice of those laity who are chosen beforehand because they will say exactly what the church leadership wants them to say), the terrible and rending birth control crisis will continue.

97

In many countries, of course, the solution that is reached is that confessors insist in theory on the official teaching, but in practice, as a concession to human weakness, tolerate contraceptive intercourse. However, such a "pastoral solution" (apparently perfectly acceptable to the Curia) offends those of us who are part of the Northern European heritage who do not want to be told that our marital love is somehow or other weak or imperfect.

One has to say that in the present situation of non-dialogue, non-discussion, and non-communication during which officials eagerly talk out of one side of their mouths to endorse the papal position and just as eagerly talk out of the other side of their mouths when dealing with the pastoral practice of the clergy, the crisis does not seem likely to be solved for a long, long time.

WHY IS THE CHURCH OPPOSED
TO HOMOSEXUALITY?

A S I understand it, the Vatican, while condemning homosexuality in theory, urges confessors to be tolerant, sympathetic
and helpful in pastoral practice. One hears it said, for example,
that seminary teachers even in Rome will say that, pastorally, a
priest should try to persuade a homosexual to have stable rather
than promiscuous relationships.

I simply don't know enough about the biology or the psychology
of the matter to go beyond the previous statement. It may be that
homosexuality is a result of genetic programming, or it may be
the result of psychological experiences or it may be a combination of both. It may be that in some instances it is "curable" and
it may be that in most instances it is not "curable." Homosexuals
ought to be treated with respect and love, they ought not to be
the objects of ridicule or discrimination. I would be very wary
of saying that any given homosexual is committing a sin—but then
I would be very wary of saying that any given heterosexual is committing a sin either, because the Scriptures tell me not to judge
lest I be judged.

However, I am not prepared to say that "gay is good" in the
sense that there is no real difference between heterosexuality and
homosexuality. I don't think that's true and I don't believe there
is any need to pretend that it is in order to support fairness and
justice for homosexuals.

Chapter Five

A Sex to Love With

TENDERNESS AND AFFECTION

THERE are two kinds of loneliness that afflict human life. The first is the loneliness that comes from the human condition. It can be mitigated and alleviated but it cannot be eliminated. The other is the loneliness that we choose freely. It can always be conquered if we choose to do so.

We are, for weal or woe, consciously individuated creatures. No love, however permanent or however powerful, makes us more than finite. We may occasionally break through the boundaries of our finitude in moments of ecstasy. But these moments experienced in mystic contemplation or at the height of sexual arousal are fleeting, and we find ourselves all too quickly alone again, cut off, isolated. Genital love even at its most rewarding does not eliminate finitude though it can be a powerful motivation for temporarily achieving union. It alleviates, however transiently, the pain and isolation of finitude, and that is all that can be asked of it. Even the most ecstatic of experiences still leaves one lonely because it still leaves one finite. It is in these experiences that man feels most poignantly his hunger for the infinite. That there is an Infinite, incidentally, does not seem a matter for doubt during or immediately after moments of ecstasy. Such confidence in the Infinite is not, I think, exactly a "proof" that there is a Lover "out there" who will be able to end our loneliness. It rather reassures us of the existence of that love. It may well be the most important reassurance.

In addition to such existential loneliness, there is also the loneliness we freely choose. Even if man may not break completely with his finitude and isolation, his life is filled with opportunities to move beyond the barriers of individuation to find psychological and physical union with others. The pleasures and delights of life and love are obvious and demanding. Our bodies and our spirits are designed to seek union with others, but the design does not

103

deprive us of our freedom. We can turn away from others; we can permit ourselves to be permanently rebuffed by them; we can lose our nerve, our courage, our imagination, our capacity for surprise. We can settle for a dull, monotonous, isolated, drab existence. We can do these things despite the primal thrust for union of body and spirit which is at the core of our personalities. To some extent, all of us choose this path of loneliness. One's giving and taking is always imperfect and inadequate. We are distracted, worried, anxious; and love is a very incomplete effort. What is important, however, is not perfection but persistence—a continuation of efforts to succumb to desire, to break out of fears, to become vigorous, challenging, surprising lovers. Even if their efforts seem to involve loss of dignity and propriety and leave them open to ridicule, lovers must persist.

Our existential loneliness is part of the human condition. Any celibate who thinks that if he had a spouse his life would have meaning and purpose and that he would be able to escape the finitude and imperfection that plagues him is naive about both sexuality and meaning. How we interpret sexual experience is not at all dictated by the experiences themselves. Nor does sexuality remove the pains of isolation and individuation for very long. It does provide us with powerful motives and powerful rewards for not surrendering to isolation and withdrawing permanently behind the impenetrable barriers of loneliness. But a man whose life has no meaning before he finds a mate, who is mired down in his own distrust and suspicion, will find neither purpose nor cure for his loneliness amid the delights a woman's body offers. She is made to be enjoyed (as, indeed, a man is made to be enjoyed), but joy does not give faith and it does not heal fear. It may give a greater reason for faith and a more powerful drive against fear, but by itself pleasure is no cure for the sickness of spirit.

What sexuality does make possible—and in this respect the sexuality need not be genital—is affection and tenderness. And perhaps in the final analysis this is what women and men most need and most want in their lives. Orgasms are nice, but affection and tenderness are indispensable. A lover does indeed provide delight, but he also protects, provides care, and helps to avoid discouragement, weariness, and boredom. No lover can eliminate these things from his (or her) life unless he (or she) is willing to fight them; but in moments when the fight seems scarcely worth the effort, the lover can show that it is. It is precisely in these moments that human love is most rewarding, most pleasurable, and most important. Whoever loves and whatever be the nature of this love, if the lover knows when to say the kind word and to apply the gentle touch, when to laugh and smile, when to encouarge and to show solicitude, when to sympathize with frustrations and to ridicule hesitancies, then the lover has immense power.

The need for affection of this kind is specifically human. It occurs only in creatures capable of reflection and who have devised symbols that give meaning to their behavior. But because affection is uniquely human, it becomes the indispensable prerequisite for human love. No matter how skilled the eroticism or genitality of lovers may be, if they do not make love in an atmosphere permeated by affection and tenderness, then their love will not be humanly satisfying. Man wants pleasure, of course, but he wants with it reassurance and comfort, and if these qualities are absent the pleasure really isn't all that much fun. The most delightful lovemaking between married couples is precisely that which is explicitly designed to alleviate loneliness, discouragement, and weariness. It is then that love most effectively communicates to the other that he is worth something, that he is desired, admired, and loved. The wife comes to distract her husband from the worries of his work with herself and the martini pitcher. She is saying that however serious the work problems may be and however much he may be discouraged, it has nothing to do with his own goodness and desirability. She loves him and wants him no matter what happens, and she is willing to engage in "shameless" behavior to make it as clear as possible to him how much she wants him and how important he is to her no matter what else happens.

And a husband who gently calms his wife at the end of what

was for her a nerve-racking, compulsive, and distracting day is telling her in effect that even if she feels she has failed to meet all of the multitudinous responsibilities that she could have coped with in the course of the day, she is still his and the source of constant delight to him not because of what she accomplished today but because of who she is. As the nightgown slips from her body, she knows not merely that she can give pleasure but also that she is a person who is cared for. That makes both the pleasure she gives and receives more intense.

Perhaps the reason for much of the infidelity that occurs in the early middle years of life is precisely that tenderness and affection have gone out of the marriage. It has become a series of obligations and responsibilities. Career (for one or for both), children, social life, political involvement, intellectual concerns—all of these use up time and energy, and while the two people still have intercourse with each other, it becomes more of a mechanical ritual than an act of reassurance and affection.

It is at just such times that a person most obviously needs affection and is most likely to attract it from others. Similary, at such times affection offered or even available can become irresistible. One gets into an affair not so much for genital release (though that is surely to be had), not so much for erotic excitement (though that is certainly present), but so that one might experience a few moments of tenderness and reassurance. One may even know that such reassurance and affection is transient, shallow, and deceptive. Nonetheless, in times of loneliness and discouragement even shallow reassurance and transient affection will be eagerly accepted when nothing else is available.

In other instances, husband and wife withhold affection from each other not because they are thoughtless or distracted but because they deliberately intend to punish each other. The inevitable conflict between them is not faced but repressed; desire is converted into anger and delight into vindictiveness. All the slights, the insensitivities, the disappointments, and the frustrations build up and affection is refused precisely at the times when it is most obviously needed. Heaven help the other person if in desperation he turns to someone else for affection, because that provides even more grounds for punishment.

The vindictive withholding of affection (and one can concede one's body without offering affection) is one of the most ugly things a man or a woman can do. In the strict sense of the word, it is hateful. In the old days, Catholic women used to feel constrained to confess when they had refused their "marital duty." What they meant, of course, was that they had refused to have intercourse with their husbands, but the "marital duty," or indeed the duty of any love, goes far beyond physical union. What really ought to be confessed before God and men is the refusal to offer tenderness, affection, reassurance, and comfort to our lover at times when he or she most clearly needs it. There are times, of course, when people can be excused for not having intercourse, but there are no times, so long as there is anything left of the relationship, when they can be excused from tenderness and comfort.

It is man's loneliness and his need for affection that make possible those two difficult and pleasurable experiences between lovers, reconciliation and new beginnings. Not all conflict can be routinized; not all problems can be resolved. Confrontation may lead to a breakdown in the relationship, and fear may so impede communication that lovers become strangers. To begin again means to admit one's past mistakes, accept responsibility for one's failures, write off all the wasted time, and go back, as it were, to ground zero to begin again. Such a wiping clean of the slate, which involves both forgiving the other and oneself, is not an easy task. A married couple in their late thirties or early forties will be greatly humiliated to admit to each other that their genital life is dull and always has been. It will be tough for the man to concede that he has been inept and clumsy in his attempts to give pleasure to his wife. It will be hard for her to admit that part of the reason for his clumsiness has been her silence and another part of it has been that she long since gave up trying to be seductive. They must go back to the beginning and pretend that they are newlyweds, or, perhaps more appropriately, that they are engaged in an illicit love affair. Indeed, by the standards of the routine to which their life together has sunk, any change will look like an illicit love affair. Each new beginning will not be easy, for it will mean that two people have learned from the mistakes that occurred in their relationship without holding these mistakes against each other. There are delights in reconciliation, of course, and a love affair which begins for the first time or anew at forty can be infinitely more pleasurable than one that begins at eighteen, for both lovers have much more experience, both physical and psychological, to bring to their affair. The past can be an asset as well as a liability, particularly if the lovers are able to develop a capacity to laugh at the grotesqueries of their past mistakes. They had better be able to laugh, because that is the only thing that will exorcise the anger and the humiliation of those mistakes.

It is the need for affection and reassurance that is the most powerful motivation for beginning anew. Most lovers cannot or will not end their relationship unless it has become completely intolerable. There are too many things at stake. It is much better to stumble along in an unsatisfactory relationship than risk the public conflict, complication, and disgrace that would come from ending it. While extramarital interludes may provide temporary affection and reassurance, they tend to become unsatisfactory in the long run. One will find comfort and affection with one's spouse or probably not at all. Of course, there is a strong strain toward renewing affection because the couple have been lovers before, and are still, to some greater or lesser extent.

What has happened is that love and hatred have been powerfully intermixed in their relationship. The ambivalence that is involved in every intimacy is now both a serious problem and a last opportunity. The man and woman really do not like each other very much and have stored up all sorts of resentments. On the other

108

hand, there are strong ties that unite them, and they can on occasion provide each other with both reassurance and pleasure.

In most marriages that have grown cool if not cold, there is in both people a latent desire to begin again, though, unfortunately, they have grown skilled in ignoring the cues that the other emits about the possibility of starting anew. What is required to begin a reconciliation is that when one person sees a tentative sign of affection and reassurance from the other, he or she should quickly respond with similar affection. There is, of course, considerable risk in either offering or responding to affection offered in a relationship that has become routine if not cool. In a way, it is an even bigger risk than beginning a love relationship, for now one knows all the things that can go wrong, and one also knows that if one attempts to renew a relationship and the other turns him down, it will make matters worse instead of better. Unfortunately, offers for renewal are frequently turned down. No one suspects that if such offers are firm enough, persistent enough, and imaginative enough, they will ultimately become irresistible in most cases.

A reconciliation involves winning a husband or wife all over again. It can be an exhilarating, fascinating, fun-filled experience. Indeed, any good marriage is a never-ending series of reconciliations. The more frequent the minor ones, the less need there will be to go through the pain of having a love relationship hit rock bottom before it begins to be reborn.

It frequently seems to those who are presented with an opportunity to begin again, to rebuild a relationship, that they are being asked to do something heroic and extraordinary. Winning each other all over again in the middle years of life seems ludicrous and absurd and simply not the thing to do. If, despite the evidence of realistic common sense, two people do begin anew, each of them may feel that what they are doing ought to be greatly rewarded. In a way they are correct. What they are doing is heroic and the rewards may very well be great, but any other course is

109

the sheerest sort of folly. One either seeks reconciliation or settles down to a life of drab, affectionless routine in which there is no excitement, no tenderness, no affection, no reassurance. Our whole existence ought to be a constant refusal of such an alternative. No matter how much humiliation and forgiveness are involved, we must not choose loneliness.

SEX, GROWTH AND PLAYFULNESS

THE *Playboy* centerfold is an erotic picture, crudely, grossly erotic, and appeals primarily to adolescent sexual fantasies. The larger the body organs, the more sexual pleasure is promised. By her smile, her deportment, her casual invitation, the Playmate of the Month promises a fun-filled romp. No hang-ups, no involvements, no commitments, no furniture to buy, no risk of being tied down, no extra responsibilities just fun and games now, as soon as you want, however you want it, whenever you want it. Images of play are there for the asking; one just has to plunk down a dollar. (If you are a woman, you have now achieved the marvelous equality of being able to plunk down your dollar for a copy of *Playgirl*.)

Let us leave aside the traditional concern over whether the *Playboy* centerfold is a "dirty" picture. (My own guess is that there are things to be found on the walls of the Vatican Museum and the ceiling of the Sistine Chapel that are more erotic.) Whatever the deficiencies the centerfolds of *Playboy* and *Playgirl* may have as part of the ancient tradition of erotic art, one must still observe that the play they promise is phony. First, the buxom young woman is not in fact prepared to play with anyone. She is posing for a picture for money and the considerable amount of fame and attention it will bring. She is not prepared to play with the cameraman taking her picture or the *Playboy* buyer who stares at her goggle-eyed. The invitation in her eyes, her smile, and the arrangement of her body may be an invitation to fantasy, but it is not in fact anything but an invitation to look. Looking may be fun, but it's not all that much fun. The *Playboy* philosophy, in fact, considers sex to be a spectator sport where participation is fantasy. The pro football fan not only admires Fran Tarkenton's ability to throw a pass, but he also identifies with him on the field. In fantasy he leaves his seat in front of the TV and descends to the gridiron and

111

the battle being played out there. Similarly, the sexual spectator projects himself into the scene depicted in the centerfold and becomes involved in the actual game of sex to which the Playmate of the Month is inviting him.

A spectator sport may be diverting, but it is no substitute for the excitement of the real thing. It is also—and this is the point— much easier than the real thing. One can fantasize that one is Fran Tarkenton and still be woefully out of shape physically and unwilling to accept the pain or the possibility of losing. Every fan in the grandstand can be a great quarterback in dream life and it requires no discipline, no practice, no suffering at all. Similarly, one can play with the Playmate of the centerfold without ever having to practice or suffer the pain and discipline of acquiring skill as an effective player in the sexual game.

All the Playmate has to do is pose and smile. When one has overcome the embarrassment of it, it is a relatively easy task. There is no need to master the skills that the pose and smile imply. The Playmate of the Month looks playful, but in the real world she could be frigid, uninterested in men, terrified of sex, bitchy, or just plain blah in bed. The tease, the pose, the smile of the Playmate may be great for the reader's fantasy life and it may even make some marginal contribution to her own, but it has little relevance for anybody's sex life. It's not the phoniness that bothers us so much—that, after all, is an element in fantasy which concerns itself with the unreal, the puffed up, the make-believe. It is the pretense that this is what play is all about that rings so false.

To be a playmate or to have a playmate is at least as difficult in its own order as being a professional quarterback. There are people who *look* like quarterbacks (and the Chicago Bears usually recruit them), but they haven't got what it takes. Strong arms, strong legs they may possess; and with the uniform and equipment they look great on the sports pages. But when the chips are down, it is the old bald men like Y. A. Tittle, grey-haired men like George Blanda, overweight men like Sunny Jurgensen and

Bobby Lane, or sore-armed bandits like Johnny Unitas and John Haidel, or thin washed-out characters like Fran Tarkenton who score the final touchdown. It is not enough to look like a quarter-back; one must be one. It is not enough to look like a Playmate; one must be good at playing.

To have a playmate means to be in possession of someone who has become a specialist in your physiology-psychology-fantasy life. It means that you belong to someone who has devoted long years and much practice to understanding you and reading you and is perfectly happy continuing to practice and perfect his skills. It means that you have yielded yourself to the other's power and influence. To permit someone else to be your playmate is a delightful yet terrifying experience. As Martin D'Arcy pointed out long ago, love is not so much possessing as being possessed. Only the brave can permit themselves to be possessed. Your partner becomes the playmate when you have become brave enough to permit the partner to possess you. And when this happens there is no way out of the commitment. The question of the permanency of commitment becomes theoretical and irrelevant. When the kind of possession required for sexual playfulness has occurred, there is no way out; one does not want to get out, and even the thought of it is absurd. There may still be conflict and tension in the relationship; indeed, any relationship between humans will certainly generate some conflict. But being possessed by a playmate also means being obsessed by him (or her). As one young married man put it, "Murder? Yes! Divorce? Don't be silly!"

Sexual playfulness, then, begins in earnest only when one has given oneself to another so totally that there is simply no way back. In the fantasy of playing with the centerfold sex object the emphasis is almost always on what the spectator does to and with the body so invitingly displayed on the foldout. In real life, playfulness means what one is willing to permit the other to do to oneself. The male who indulges in his late adolescent fantasies with Playmate of the Month might very well be paralyzed with terror

113

if the woman whose picture attracts him should stride into his real life and demand the kind of influence, power, and control over him that real life playmates must have if the game is to begin.

Similarly, the modern liberated woman who joins the growing ranks of those who buy *Playgirl* may shiver with anticipation at the fantasies which arise from the promises of the magazine. But in real life she is most reluctant to yield as much of herself to a man as would be required to make those fantasies anything but daydreams. A man as strong and as demanding and as resourceful and as persistent as the one in the centerfold would scare the living daylights out of her.

Real playmates are scary people, because they want us body and soul. If we give ourselves to them they will indeed provide all the pleasure and happiness they promise, but there will be fear and suffering in the constant struggle to become more fully possessed and to more fully possess. The centerfold characters—male or female—promise everything and demand nothing. Real playmates demand everything, and they are not satisfied until they get it. They learn only slowly and with difficulty how to effectively demand everything from us; and we learn only slowly and with difficulty how to respond to their demands. Both the playmate and the one with whom he (or she) plays acquire the skills of the game only with effort after mistakes, miscues, false starts, and failures.

Having a playmate and being one are reciprocal phenomena. Another person will be a playmate for us to the extent that we are fierce and determined enough to take possession of the other even as he (or she) is possessing us. We must be a specialist in the other's physiology-psychology-fantasy in the same way the other is a specialist in ours. There are no short cuts, no easy way out, no manuals to explain how to do it, no weekend courses to give us a degree validating our sexual playfulness. A good deal of the coin of the realm can be accumulated by those who write books and run weekend sessions on sex. There is titillation in them and the satisfaction that comes from feeling one is enlightened and a member of the avant garde—so perhaps those who read and attend get their money's worth. To give the sex manuals and the encounter movement the most I will concede to them, a little bit may happen to those involved in them in a few cases. But, in general, attempts to short circuit the long, slow difficult road to possession and being possessed may be fun but they are fundamentally counterfeit. They frequently reinforce the fears, the anxiety, the game-playing, the hiding behind masks that enable so many couples to escape the terrors of playing in the sexual game.

One of the principal obstacles to sexual play is the myth of competence. The assumption of the "Playboy Philosophy" and of more sophisticated forms of contemporary hedonism is that the spectator is already competent. Show a man the Playmate of the Month and he knows what to do to her; show a woman the centerfold of *Playgirl* and she knows how to react. Indeed, *Playboy* (and to a lesser and derivative extent, *Playgirl*, too) constantly flatters their readers by assuring them of their indubitable, unquestioned sexual omnicompetence. It's nice to be told we're good in bed, because we know we should be but have the sinking feeling that we are not.

Most adults know how babies are born. They know how sexual organs are made to be linked, and under appropriate circumstances they can perform the indicated operation with a certain minimum amount of efficiency. If that were all that is required to be an effective lover, then almost everyone would be sexually competent. Fears of sexual inadequacy that assail most of us would have no meaning at all.

But sex is between people, not merely between bodies. People are different; one can reach orgasm with a prostitute, but one can only play with another human whom he knows. And that brings us up against the mystery of another person's self.

Lock a man in a room with a Playmate of the Month and tell him he must make love to her. He will be sexually aroused, of course, but he will also be terrified because now he faces a real woman—attractive, mysterious, complex, baffling, able to respond at the promptings of herself, not only *his* fantasies. He can force himself crudely and brutally upon her and achieve the basic release that comes from orgasm; but this is not what his masculine ego and self-confidence demand of him. The interlude with this beautiful woman must be an event to remember, not just a few quick physiological spasms. She must enjoy it as much as he does. The totality of both their persons must be involved in a memorable and thoroughly satisfying experience. She is waiting for him to begin. What does she want? How should he start? How should they do it? How long should they prepare? What kind of foreplay would be best? What will really turn her on? What kinds of tenderness and affection will be most reassuring and stimulating? What can he do to make her respect and admire him? How can it be the kind of event that will make her want more of the same? How can he impress her as a sexually imaginative, creative, competent male? It is as though he has been put in the huddle of the Minnesota Vikings and called upon to deliver the game-winning pass when he can't even remember the game plan. Under such circumstances not a few men would become impotent and many others would simply turn into brutes. They are put into a situation where sexual competence is demanded of them immediately, and they simply do not know what to do.

Put a woman in the same situation where she is imprisoned with an extraordinarily attractive male who makes it perfectly clear that he is willng to make love. In her fantasy life she had dreamed repeatedly of having such a splendid male body available, but now she simply does not know what to do. Does he really find her attractive? Is she too thin or too fat? Are her sex organs too big or too small? Can she really hold his attention and interest? What should they talk about? How should she begin? What should she do with her hands and her mouth? What kinds of things would he like her to do to her? Why is she so frightened? Is she frigid?

The point is, of course, that no matter how attractive we are

116

we feel incompetent with strangers. It may be possible to do the bare minimum, although a man frightened into impotency by a strange encounter may not be able to do even that. Sexual competency is not a generalized ability, save for a few simple and easily learned physiological movements. It is an interpersonal competency gained with this particular person who happens to be our sexual partner at this particular segment of the space-time continuum. The stranger can't be a playmate because he (or she) doesn't know us and we don't know him. An interlude with a stranger may be successful enough to achieve mutual orgasmic relase, and there may be a lucky occasion or two when strangers discover important physiological characteristics about one another quickly enough to heighten the pleasure of the experience. But the payoff declines rapidly, because there is far more in sexual play than the tension release of orgasm, however spectacular it may be. The strangers may become playmates, but they do so by exactly the same long, slow process of discovering the totality of one another's selfhood that occurs in any sustained sexual commitment. There is no reason, in other words, why this particular man and this particular woman should expect immediate sexual competency with one another. On the contrary, if they are wise they will expect a lifelong growth in mutual competency. And if they are already well into their marriage, they are simply deceiving themselves if they have become convinced that they are so competent with one another that there is nothing more to learn. Interpersonal sexual competency can be said to only begin when a couple has been together for a considerable amount of time. If we were just animals, that would not be the case. But we are human animals with fears, anxieties, needs, longings, and, above all, complex systems of meaning which interpret for us all the events of our life, particularly those that challenge us most directly as men and women. The real playmate is one who has achieved a high degree of competency in dealing with us because he (or she) shares our body, our spirit, our fantasy-life and our meaning systems. When we are put into a room with such a person and told that we have nothing else to do but make love, questions of competency are quite irrelevant.

Hence the esssential prerequisite for growth in playfulness is the admission that we are not competent automatically and that we have to grow and learn what competency means with this other person. It is a hard admission to make, hard at the beginning of marriage and even harder as the years go on. For a man to admit to his wife, "I don't really know you. I don't really know how to make love to you," is a shattering experience. (Of course, it need not be expressed in those words.) For a woman to say to her husband, "You are a mystery to me. I have no real notion of how to please and satisfy you" is also shattering. Such admissions are an acceptance of the necessity for trust, confidence, respect, and affection to be established in some amount at least as an atmosphere conducive to the growth of sexual competence and playfulness. You can only admit that you are not good at something in the presence of another who is already sufficiently impressed by you that your admission of incompetence is not likely to diminish his respect for you. One can admit incompetence in most cases only in a set of circumstances where one can be reasonably confident that the other will increase rather than decrease his respect for you precisely because of the admission. If the man is convinced that when he says to his wife that he does not really understand how to make her happy, she will love him more, not less, his concesssion becomes relatively easy—though still painful. A woman will find it much easier to tell her husband that she needs to know much more about what is required to bring him pleasure (in bed and in the rest of their relationship) if she knows that his love will be deepened by such a request.

In other words, when we admit our lack of competence and our inadequacies in circumstances where there is already love and affection, then we are engaged precisely in that process of self-disclosure and self-revelation which is already erotic play. The confession of inadequacy and the desire to learn is already an act of sexual playfulness—and in the proper circumstances an intensely erotic one. "Show me how" is just about the most seductive thing one can say to his sexual partner, yet the words are so hard to say, they stick rigidly in our throat.

Playfulness also requires the freedom to learn by mistakes, failures, and trial and error. If the whole relationship depends on the success of every experiment, then playfulness doesn't have much of a life expectancy. A woman reads that a sheer black bra will turn a man on, so she buys the naughtiest one she can find and gives her husband a good, long look at her in it one evening. He seems mildly interested in how much it cost, but is not aroused at all. If he were really sensitive, he would of course catch what she was trying to do and respond enthusiastically, if not to the garment, at least to her. No one is sensititve to every cue all the time. If this failure so discourages the woman that she is unwilling to risk other "naughty" experiments, then there is simply not enough trust and playfulness in the relationship for the awkward trial and error growth, which is the only way playfulness can expand and develop.

Similarly, a man finds himself intrigued by what he has heard of some of the "French" techniques of combining lovemaking and powerlessness. He explains the techniques to his wife and she shows a mild interest. They experiment and discover that the experience is considerably less for them than the wild, incredible pleasure the sex manuals promised. Both are bound to be somewhat disappointed, but if they can laugh the incident off and add it to the growing list of shared jokes the fund of trust and playfulness is great enough for their continued expansion and growth.

Techniques are relatively unimportant when compared with the fundamental dynamics of a relationship. Two human beings living in what is frequently oppressive intimacy make mistakes in dealing with each other every day. A thoughtless word, a joke that is intended to be funny but is cutting and is hurtful, a burst

119

of exasperation at the wrong time, a trivial complaint when tenderness is needed—these can be either laughed off or become part of the hidden agenda of frustration, anger and bitterness. Playfulness in bed and playfulness in the totality of a relationship mutually reinforce one another. Genital sexuality that is rigid and unimaginative inhibits the growth of playfulness in the common life, and a common life that is grim, serious, "responsible" and filled with mistakes, reprimands, and temper tantrums is not going to be transformed into play when the bedroom door closes.

Play is competitive. There is a certain kind of do-gooding mentality in the United States that thinks competition is Capitalist Immorality and that little children should learn to cooperate with one another instead of competing. Competition is part of the vitality of life. Little children compete and cooperate simultaneously in their games. They cannot compete unless they set up a framework of cooperation, and it is the enjoyment and challenge of competition that encourages them to sustain and improve the cooperation that provides the context of the game. What is wrong is the belief that you have to win all the time for the competition to be worth the effort. If the only fun in the game is winning, the game isn't much fun at all. No one can will all the time, and people who equate losing the game with failure in a wider sense miss the point of competition completely. (Incidentally, I find grammar school athletic programs repellent. Pick-up contests, sandlot games, ad hoc confrontations on the playing fields are great fun and part of growing up for both boys and girls. Well organized, uniformed, efficiently coached operations—like Little League, for example— are a serious business and designed more for parents than as healthy sport for children. These contests are so important to the parent because he, having lost all sense of playfulness, equates losing a game with failure in the real world.)

Part of the fun of the game is its competitiveness. "I top you, you top me;" "I'm better than you are, you're better than I am;" "I can do something you can't do, you can do something I can't do.'' Indeed, the more fiercely competitive the game, the more fun it is for both sides because the more it challenges both to their maximum efforts. Only when the rules of the game are violated and the norms of the outside world are brought in does loss mean failure and defeat mean ignominy. Then, of course, one of the players will end the game and go home.

When a man and woman are cramped together in the narrow life space of their marriage there will be competition and conflict as they spar together for relative advantage over the limited resources that are available to them. Such conflict and competition are ways of working out tensions, of balancing needs, and of strengthening the bonds that hold the joint venture together. If the competition can be approached with the playfulness of the game world, where the competition is real indeed but not "serious" in the sense that the fundamental ego-strength and indispensable needs of either partner are being violated, then the bonds of cooperation are strengthened. They struggle together in order that they may struggle together. They contend with each other the way Jacob did with the angel of Yahweh, not in anger, not to tear the relationship apart, but in order to bind it together more solidly. The wrestling match between Jacob and the angel of Yahweh was indeed a wrestling match. God and Jacob were contending, fighting, competing with one another, but it was a competition that grew out of love and re-enforced that love.

Sexual competitiveness is indescribably erotic. If each partner is struggling to be better than the other sexually, it necessarily means that each is struggling to be better at giving pleasure to the other rather than taking it for oneself. It is the kind of competition in which everybody wins. If the husband has a particularly good night, in which his wife is at first reluctant and resistant and ends up almost pathetically pleading for more, he has won but so has she. If the wife drives out of her husband's mind all distractions, all thoughts of other women, indeed everything but desire for her by a scene that will haunt him for several days, she has triumphed indeed, but he has not exactly been a loser. To win a point in the sexual game is an absolute delight. "I showed him" or "I showed her" is a cry of exultation and self-satisfaction, but to lose a point by being shown is also a memorable experience.

Competition in the sexual game becomes unhealthy only under two circumstances: either one of the partners won't play, or one of the partners refuses to let the other play. In both cases all points are scored on one side, and the other is reduced, by his choice or by his partner's, to playing the role of passive cooperator. He becomes a respondent and audience who must react to and applaud the triumphs of the perennial victor. Some men's sexual egos are so weak that this is the only kind of game they are capable of playing. Their relationship with a woman must be an endless series of "scores." Some women are so prudish, so passive, or so frightened that "to win" a sexual tussle with a man would be to deny their femininity. Such children, the conquering male and the ever-conquered female, may blend together in a stable relationship, and presumably worse things could happen to them. The man might have married a woman who insists on "scoring " sometimes herself, and she might have married a man who wants to be challenged as well as applauded and accepted. But such stable, routine, one-way relationships ought not to be confused with playfulness. Nobody wants to play golf with the pro who shoots in the low 70s unless he plays with an equalizing handicap. Sexual competitiveness between a husband and wife enhances the sex gain only when there is relative equality between the contestants, which means that the husband must be brave enough to lose some of the encounters and the wife brave enough to win some of them.

The very use of the words "win" and "lose" will be offensive to some. How can one speak of winning and losing in something as intimate and private as human love? It is not difficult if one remembers that in the world of the game one's success or failure as a human or as a man or woman is in no way connected to whether one wins or loses the game. The equations winning =

success, losing = failure are an invasion of the world of the game by norms and values that do not belong there. A husband and wife, involved in a deeply affectionate and playful sexual relationship with each other will have no problem at all understanding what I mean. The husband has many times experienced self-satisfaction, pride, and complacency as he drops off to sleep thinking "I really did it to her tonight," while the wife is falling asleep happily overwhelmed by an aggressive, demanding, absolutely implacable lover. Tonight she lost, but she had as much fun losing as he did winning.

For a woman to think to herself that this was her night for victory may well be even more exciting and rewarding than it would be for her husband. For in the culture in which she was raised, winning in sex is a male prerogative. To be able to win at the game is to show both the culture and her husband. She can be weak, passive, and surrendering when that is appropriate; she can be as fierce, demanding, impassioned, and as implacable as he when that is her mood.

Perhaps the most pleasurable kind of sexual play comes on those occasions when both the man and the woman are in aggressive, implacable moods. The competition then is indeed a fierce fight; it is Jacob wrestling with the angel of Yahweh. The struggle is wild, passionate, terrifying, indescribably enjoyable. Which of the partners "wins" may ultimately depend on the fine-tuned sensitivity of the other. If they are really skillful players at the sexual game they will be able to know when the other really ought to win, when at the last moment one substitutes graceful surrender for continued conflict. This is, of course, sexual playfulness refined to a high art. But the nice thing about having a lifetime playmate is that one has a long time to refine one's skills at the art. The equations of the sexual game may be unique in the game world—losing = winning, winning = winning. That's a game to bet on!

Playmates must be strong. They must refuse to take "no" for an answer (save on those occasions when their sensitivities reveal to them that "no" is reasonable with no diminution of love and trust). The playmate must have the vigor and the resourcefulness to tear away the masks and the defenses, the protections, the phony fears—the silly anxieties—all those escape hatches one uses to flee the terrors and delights of the sexual game. Strength requires confidence, of course, and a playmate who is not confident of his or her abilities to deal effectively with a sexual partner will not be much of a playmate. Conflict can coexist with the admission that one's competency needs to grow and develop. Indeed the assertion of omni-competence is normally an attempt to hide lack of confidence. The confident playmate says in effect, "There may still be much I have to learn about my spouse's fantasies, needs, desires, responses; but I know enough to be able to begin, and I am secure enough in our relationship to be able to move ahead." Confidence means that one is strong enough, secure enough, and knowledgeable enough to begin, knowing that afterwards the "playing by ear" that inevitably follows will not be a total failure. the problem for the man locked in the room with the Playmate of the Month that we discussed earlier is that he really doesn't know how to begin. How can he, since he is dealing with a stranger? Surely the first time a couple who have committed themselves to each other come together they too lack confidence, but they can both feel brave enough, strong enough, secure enough, accepted enough, loved enough to begin. Competency grows when confidence is a given.

But it is a given that needs constant re-enforcement. If we expect our sexual partner to become a playmate for us, we must constantly support, re-enforce, and build the partner's ego strength. A man needs to be told day in and day out that he is a good lover— even on those occasions when he is only adequate. A woman needs to hear, in season and out, that she is a totally gorgeous, desirable, seductive, irresistible female—even on those occasions when her awkwardness and hesitance make her quite resistible. A partner becomes a playmate to the extent that we successfully define him (or her) as such. A man cannot hear too often from his wife that she wants his body in her; and she cannot hear too often from him that her breasts are so delectable that he simply cannot keep his hands off them.

To what extent must this pursuit of confidence and competence be explicit for the sexual game to flourish? Is it an art that can be pursued implicitly, tacitly, unreflectively? Or must it be something that is the subject of constant explicit dialogue and discussion within a relationship?

There are no clear and simple answers to these questions. Some people can develop an extraordinarily playful sexual relationship through skilled communication that is almost always subliminal and unobtrusive. Others can become easy and matter-of-fact in discussing the most intimate details of their lovemaking. Still others talk about it constantly, persuading themselves and boring others about their really great sex life when in fact they are blindly following the paradigms they find in the most recent manual. Finally, some people may be so tied in puritanical knots that they pretend most of the time that no such thing as sex exists in their life together. The style with which a couple pursues mastery of sexual playfulness depends upon the style of their personalities and the style of their relationship. Some talk too much, others not nearly enough. On balance it can be said that for most American couples the real risk is that they will not talk nearly enough.

To be "masterful" (or "mistressful") at the sexual game is to be in command of the situation, to be able to combine implacable firmness with sensitive tenderness, to know when to comfort, when to challenge, when to insist, when to defer, when to push, when to yield, when to become angry, when to reassure, when to win, when to lose, when to overwhelm, when to be overwhelmed, when to tear away resistance, and when to respect it. One can only learn these delicate arts by experimentation, practice, and attention to feedback. In the ordinary course of events most human beings gain mastery only to the extent that they focus self-conscious energy and effort on the process. It is not something that comes easily, naturally, or unreflectively.

To the argument that there are too many other obligations and responsibilities and important things in life to devote time to such a frivolous pursuit, one can only say that this is an option some people freely choose, but it is one that, in principle at least, is an obligation for no one. It may well be that there are other satisfactions in life that make sexual playfulness seem relatively unimportant. If that is the case for a given couple, so be it; but they are kidding themselves if they think that they have rejected an option that did not contain pleasure, variety, wonder, and reward. It is a good thing to be masterful, to feel that one has supreme and loving power over the other, that one can possess the other without his or her having the ability or the desire to resist. It is also good to know that one is under such tender but effective domination by another human being, that there is someone who can do with us whatever he or she wants, and that whatever he or she wants is what we want. Those who don't particularly care for such payoffs in their lives are within their rights in rejecting them, but they can scarcely dismiss as fools those who think otherwise.

A man puts his arm around his wife. She is limp, weary, depressed, and reluctant; it has been a hard day for her. His personality expands, blood rushes through his veins, his heart stirs because he knows that he has within himself the power to bring that limp body alive with pleasure and delight. It is not an absolutely necessary thing for a man to have such an experience, but it is a good thing, and for most men the more often they can have it, the better.

A woman sees her husband's face lined with care and preoccupation. There are a thousand and one troubled, anxious thoughts darting through his mind. She slips off her dress and exults in the power that is hers to so transform things that in a few moments there will be only one thing on his mind. When she is finished with him, the world will necessarily be brighter and warmer and more benign. It is not necessary for a woman to experience such exultation in her womanliness. Still it doesn't hurt, and most women cannot experience it too often. Playfulness, then, is not indispensable, but the question is why should anyone want to dispense with it?

To be playful in a sustained sexual relationship means to keep romance alive. Romance requires imagination, sympathy, understanding, persistence, sensitivity. It also requires physical tenderness. The frequency with which people make love depends on their tastes and needs. (Nine times a month is the American average, we are told.) But if physical tenderness is limited to just lovemaking, there is little romance left in the relationship. There are many times in the course of a life together when a gentle touch, a quick caress, a light kiss convey more passion, more romance, more commitment, and more playfulness than an extended romp in bed. The essence of playfulness is not so much that there is a necessity to do anything, but that there is an opportunity to do practically everything. Probably it is that absence of obligation and the presence of unlimited opportunity in sexual playfulness that must offends the puritans.

Chapter Six

Life's Answers in Religious Truths

WHAT IS THE REAL RELATIONSHIP
OF RELIGIOUS TRUTH TO LIFE?

WE HAVE been educated by methods that incline us to completely misunderstand the relationship of religious truth to human life. We come away from such educational experiences with the notion that there exists somewhere a collection of religious truths, or, if we are more up to date, religious symbols which have gathered together—perhaps in the "deposit of faith" (one gets the image of an underground vault somewhere beneath the apostolic palace of the Vatican)—and are to be applied to the human condition.

This collection of religious truths has come from some place—presumably "revelation"—and has an independent existence of its own over against human experience and by which human experience is to be interpreted, judged, explained, and validated. Religious questions, in other words, are asked out of our experience of life, and the religious answers are imposed from the outside on that experience. Revelations, we were taught implicitly, provided absolute, safe, and certain answers to life's questions.

What such a perspective overlooked were the profound psychological, sociological, and linguistic truths (emphasized especially by the great scientist and philosopher Michael Polanyi) that far more critical than the answers were the questions themselves. The wording of the question already implies the answer. The answers to most of our religious questions are in fact implicit in the questions, or at least in our ability to ask the questions.

Religious truth grows out of human experience, achieves a reality of its own when it is first of all articulated in stories or in symbols and then, only later, in philosophical propositions. Then it "bounces back" to provide explicit answers and detailed interpretations for those human experiences that are already inchoately explained and interpreted in the fact of experience itself.

131

Religion, to put the matter in somewhat different words, confirms our hunch that our wildest dreams will come true; and it ultimately takes its strength from our profound internal conviction that the hunch is right.

All this may sound new or radical or even heretical. At least it seems to be untraditional. In fact, it is quintessentially traditional. All good religious teaching (the parables of Jesus, for example) take such a perspective for granted.

But I'd still better explain. Or at least illustrate.

Let us take the renewal experience of reconciliation in which two lovers (any kind of lovers), after a long, bitter, and angry quarrel, take hesitant and stumbling first steps, then impulsive and hurried strides toward the rebirth of love. Such an experience of sorrow, forgiveness, renewal, reconciliation, and the rebirth of a more durable love are almost as intrinsic to the human condition as breathing.

If one has gone through even a few such experiences, one must begin to ask whether the reality of hatred or the reality of forgiveness and reconciliation is more powerful. Is what forgiveness stands for more powerful than that for which anger stands? Is what reconciliation stands for more powerful than that for which hatred stands? The person who has been through the renewing experience of reconciliation has not the slightest doubt. Rebirth is stronger than death, love is stronger than hate, forgiveness stronger than anger.

From that conviction—a fundamental and basic religious insight—arises our suspicion that the universe itself is animated by forgiveness, renewal, and rebirth. The religious symbol, from whatever symbol tradition, is then invoked (for the first time when a tradition begins or subsequently by those who inherit it) to articulate, confirm, reinforce, and validate the meaning of this intimate explanation, this "rumor of angels," this "signal of the transcendent," this sacrament (note the small "s") of God's love.

IS THERE SOMEONE REALLY OUT THERE?

MYTHS are true stories, not in the sense of scientifically accurate descriptions, but rather in that they are interpretations of reality cloaked in the language of the whole man and directed at the consciousness of the whole man. The neat, positivistic language of empirical science is useless for coping with the ultimate, the sacred, the transcendent. Man, therefore, turns to mythopoetic language and mythopoetic knowledge. It is with this sort of language and this sort of knowledge that he describes the relationships between God—that is to say, the Really Real—and man. But the lurking positivist in each of us still asks a gnawing question: granted that the myths describe the Really Real as personified in God, does that mean that the myth-maker *really* thinks that there is someone *out there?* The answer is that in his own level of thought and discourse the myth-maker certainly believes that there is someone out there, but he does not believe that the someone is a person in the same limited sense that we use the word in speaking of fellow human beings. What the myth-maker is trying to convey—at least if he is a Jewish or a Christian myth-maker—is that the Really Real does indeed care about us; far more in fact than we can possibly care about him. The myth-maker is saying not only that Ultimate Reality is good, but that it is benign and gracious; or as one theologian put it in the convoluted language that theologians use so as not to offend students who have had a course in introductory physics, "It would be wrong to deny to Ultimate Reality the highest attributes that we recognized in human person."

But what the myth-maker is trying to convey to those who listen to his story can be stated with considerably more bluntness: Ultimate Reality is a Thou. One need not believe this, of course. Whether one believes it or rejects it, in either event, one must make a leap of faith. But this assertion is, nevertheless, at the very

133

core of the Jewish and Christian religious traditions. The Really Real is a Thou, and a Thou who cares. If, gentle readers, you are going to reject the Christian mythology, make sure that you know what you are rejecting, because that is what the ball game is all about.

One of the most difficult and tiresome tasks for anyone who is attempting to expound the Christian message is the refusal of many men and women to go beyond quibbling over the details of the myth to face up to the reality that the myth is trying to convey. Let us take two of the more important Christian myths, the Eucharistic supper and the resurrection, as examples. The basic theme of the Last Supper mythology is, of course, that the Church is a community of friends; that Jesus is present as a friend and that friendship exists among Christians and between Christians and Jesus when they gather around the table to eat the Eucharistic banquet—the banquet which continues Jesus's work in time and space. There can be no doubt that the very earliest Christians as reported in the New Testament firmly believed that Jesus was indeed really present in the Eucharistic meal. But a vast amount of energy has been expended on explaining and debating and agonizing over the precise nature of this presence of Jesus. I do not wish to minimize the importance of theological analysis, but I simply want to make the point that it is of much less importance to be able to explain "how" the real presence occurs than it is to be able to explain what it means; yet, most of our catechetical and theological effort, particularly in the last four or five centuries, seems to have fixated on the "how" to the deemphasizing if not the complete ignoring of the "what." One can only suspect that Jesus must be somewhat chagrined. People are so busy arguing about how the Eucharist happens that they seem to have lost interest in what it means; quite possibly because what it means is so frightening.

Similarly, the obvious theme of the resurrection myth is that mankind will live; that human life will triumph over death. But much of the concern of apologetic and catechetic effort has been not to attempt to interpret and explain this fantastic conviction, but rather to develop a theory of how exactly the resurrection happened; to harmonize the various accounts in the four Gospels, and to provide satisfactory explanation to those who are worried about all the physical details. Such efforts are not an utter waste of time, but they are in the final analysis rather beside the point. In the words of Carl Braaten:

> In affirming the event of the resurrection, we are not offering a theory to explain it. What is basic to the Christian hope is that it happened and what it means, not how it happened. The urge to explain it, however, will never subside. Explanation is a dimension of understanding we always seek. Nevertheless, it would be foolish to hold that an explanation is needed to gain access to the life it promises. That would be like refusing to watch television until one could explain electricity, or refusing to admit one had fallen in love before explaining how it happened.[1]

Braaten is not saying, and neither am I, that it is unimportant whether Jesus rose from the dead or not; it is extremely important. What is more important about the resurrection of Jesus is that it represents a promise of life for all men, and what is relatively unimportant is the theory we devise to explain how the resurrection occurred.

The catechetics and the apologetics of our collective unconscious are so powerful, however, that it takes some wrenching for us to view things from such a perspective. Yet, when some bright young radical theologian announces that he no longer accepts the resurrection of Christ (and even suggests that the Apostles might

---

[1] Carl E. Braaten, *The Future of God.* New York: Harper & Row, 1969, p. 75. ©1969 by Carl E. Braaten.

really have stolen the body) we must shake our heads in dismay and assert that the bright young radical theologian has quite completely missed the point of the resurrection mythology. For the ultimate issue is whether man through Christ will triumph over death, whether the entire human race will triumph over death; for this is what the Christian message really says. If you are going to reject Christianity you may as well reject it because of its most outlandish claim, for it is much more difficult to believe that the whole race will conquer death than to believe that one man conquered death.

In other words, if one puts together the themes of the Eucharist and the resurrection and tries to find their meaning, one is forced to conclude the Christian interpretive scheme is saying that not only is the Really Real a Thou, but it is a Thou which came to us in order to assure us not merely that we could be friends, not merely that we could triumph over death, but that he would remain present among us to reinforce our friendship and to assure the triumph over death. This is, as I have said before, an outrageous and outlandish claim, but it is at the very center of the Christian interpretive scheme. If Christianity and its God are to be accepted or rejected, let them be so on those grounds and not on more trivial ones.

THERE MUST BE SOMETHING MORE

SALVATION, hope, the grace of redemption, sin, forgiveness of sin, all components of the Christian belief system, when experienced not as abstract parts of a theological system but as images and stories of a warm, passionate, forgiving God hold tremendous appeal for many who have drifted away and are at a point in life where they are experiencing a need for "something more." Indeed, the sociological evidence would seem to indicate that these concepts rather than moral pronouncements and discussions over theological detail are what bring most people back.

Our analysis of the reasons for coming home [to the Church] reveals a fact which undoubtedly applies equally to most of those who have never drifted away (save for the small minority who are personally involved in the function of the official Church or in the study of theology). The Catholic Christian faith exercises its greatest appeal when it offers a vision of life, when it inspires people to hope that with God's help they might transform their experiences and their world, when it uses the images and stories of its rich tradition to encourage people to the extraordinary behavior called for by Jesus in the Sermon on the Mount, and when it offers the hope of God's "enspiriting" us so we will be enabled individually and as a community to continue the transformative work of Jesus, that is, continue to offer his message of hope to others.

The pages of the Old and New Testament abound with stories of people searching for salvation and of God's presence in the midst of their joys and their sorrows, their good times and their bad times. The lives of ordinary people become extraordinary through the presence of God. The problems and possibilities present in experiences of marriage and family life, human sexuality, work and commitment to religious community are part of the life of the Biblical people as much as they are part of our experience today. God's presence in the Biblical stories, challenging people to live a life according to the Divine plan and not simply according to the way of the world, is a presence which the Church needs to offer to people at all times.

Indeed, the Church is the social institution entrusted with the task of carrying on the transformative mission of Jesus, that is, to present a vision that will inspire people to live lives according to the Divine plan. We are not simply to follow rules, regulations and guidelines because they are required for membership in a social institution, but we are to commit ourselves to developing an appreciation of how in our own life best to live according to the Divine plan.

THE TRINITY:

THE Catholic Christian religious symbol which indicates that God is relational in an ongoing process of knowledge and love. In the old days we thought of the Trinity as a bafflement to test our faith. Recently we discovered the fact that mysteries aren't dark puzzles to torment us but dazzling shafts of light which blind us by their brilliance. The mystery of the triune God is the mystery of God as relational process, God as ongoing knowledge and love.

THE KINGDOM OF HEAVEN

A ND you are lying on the beach," intoned the hypnotist-analyst in her rich Viennese accent, "and you are at peace. Six angels appear, and they are strong, handsome angels with great wings and flowing white robes. They lift you up, up, up into the air, and you are transported up into the sky, through the clouds into heaven."

By now I was deep in the trance, and the hypnotist's power of suggestion was receding into the background. My own unconscious was taking over. The angels lost their wings, their white robes, and their angelic faces, appearing in rough brown and green garments. And they weren't carrying me; we were striding down a forest road on a spring morning, singing great marching songs as we went and laughing as we sang. We came to a top of a knoll, and there the forest ended. We looked out over a great, sprawling city which did not, to tell the truth, look anything like the book of Revelations. It glittered white in the sun, indeed, but it was no mysterious Oriental city. It was a great, bustling, modern metropolis with skyscrapers and rapid transit and moving vehicles and streams of people moving to and fro. Beyond its towering skyline there glittered a great, smooth blue lake. It was a place, my vigorous escorts informed me, to which I could not go quite yet, but they assured me that it was there; and it was a great, splendid city, was it not? Perhaps the most striking thing in the city was its activity. I would not call it frantic, but it was alive with activity. It glittered not with rich marble or soft pastels but with sharp, bright, active, vital colors. Slowly the vision receded and I rose out of the trance.

"But a very strange thing happened," said the hypnotist. "When the angels were lifting you into the sky you were solemn and serious, and you had a very 'religious' look on your face. But then when you were deep into the trance the look changed, and it was almost as though what you saw was funny, almost as though you were enjoying a great joke. Indeed you had the expression of a little boy who is doing something very wicked by delightfully watching something he wasn't supposed to see at all. It did not seem to me," she concluded, "to be a very religious experience for you at all."

I guess it depends on what you mean by religious. It clearly was not a vision of floating around on clouds with winged, white-robed, harp-playing angels. It was not a glorious Byzantine city all solemn and sacred in gold and marble. If you believe that God is a comedian and the Holy Spirit is a leprechaun, you can't think of heaven as a very solemn, sober, and dull place.

I am sure that when my unconscious took over I combined Robin Hood's merry men tramping through Sherwood Forest with my first sight of San Francisco from the Twin Peaks and Chicago's lakefront seen at sunrise on a clear spring morning. That, at least, is what my unconscious thinks heaven is like, and on balance it strikes me that it couldn't be any better.

But imagine your own heaven if you will. If it is to be a Christian heaven, you can dispense with the Greek image of people sitting around plucking musical instruments and not doing much else but look vapid. The Christian heaven is active, dynamic, vigorous. It is not a place where life ends but rather a place where it continues.

In one sense it is not at all difficult to imagine what life after death will be like, for it will be like life as we know it here on earth. It will be filled with the excitement, the wonder, the pleasures, the activity that make life rewarding and exciting here on earth. Any sharp discontinuity between the two forms of life is completely foreign, I think, to the Christian resurrection symbolism. It was the same Jesus on Easter as before, transformed perhaps, glorious perhaps, but still Jesus. So it is with us, we believe, and the transformation will destroy nothing that is good or true or beautiful about human life. On the contrary, it will merely enhance what we already are.

On the other hand, we cannot even begin to imagine what our continued life will be like. Jesus himself has told us this: "Eye has not seen, nor has ear heard, nor has it entered into the heart of man those things which God has prepared for those who love Him." Our expectations, according to Maeterlinck, are all too modest. It will be life as we know it here on earth, but so transformed that we cannot even begin to imagine how splendid it will be. "Dream your most impossible dreams, hope your wildest hopes, fantasize your most impossible fantasies," Jesus tells us. "Then where they leave off, the surprises of my heavenly Father will only begin."

So we can look forward to both continuity and discontinuity, continuity of life but extraordinary transformation of the quality, the intensity, the richness, the splendor of life. It sounds like quite a show.

Most certainly this continued life of ours will be marked by surprises and by wonder. It is hard to imagine any kind of human life without surprises and wonder. If we have lost the little child's capacity to delight in surprise, to be awed by the wonder, we have not become adult; we have become aged and senile. The fullness of life requires a highly sensitive awareness of the possibility of surprise and a powerful capacity for wonder. If life persistent is to be life at all, then it must be life filled with surprises and wonder. John Shea's comment that the Chrisitan prepares for death by developing his capacity for surprise is strictly and literally true. One simply cannot make it in the heavenly kingdom unless one is able to cope with surprise. Perhaps that's what Purgatory is all about; it's a place where we are given the chance to make up for the sense of wonder we did not develop and the capacity for surprise that we permitted to atrophy here on earth. Purgatory would then be less a place of suffering and more a place of preparation, a kind of spring training camp where we can learn to enjoy the wonderful, the marvelous, the unexpected.

Will hopefulness continue in the heavenly kingdom? That which is most authentically human in us is our hope. It is what enables us, forces us, to ask the religious questions and gives us the most powerful hint we have of the religious answers. It is that which most enables us to be ourselves, to release the full, rich, and vigorous potentialities of our personality, to take risks, to ask not why, but why not?

Will we have dispensed with hope when we come to the many mansions of the heavenly Father's kingdom?

The old catechetics said that we would, arguing that when one has achieved one's goal there is nothing left to hope for. Certainly St. Paul implied as much in his famous quotation in the first epistle to the Corinthians, chapter 13.

If one restricts hope to the human ability to assert that death is not the final answer, that when all the evil things that are possible have been done to us there is still yet one more word to be said, then obviously there is no more need for hope after that answer and after that last word. But hope can also mean a confidence of further growth, development, expansion, a challenge to more activity, a readiness for new adventures, an openness to new wonders. It is very hard to see how there can be human life without this kind of hope. So hope in this sense, or, as the sociologists would say, some kind of functional substitute for what we would call hope in our present state of life, would surely persist in our continued life after the transition point of death.

On the psychological level, I would suggest that what we will experience in our continued life will be what my colleague Mihaly Csikszentmihalyi calls "flow." He means that experience we enjoy when our capacities and talents are pushed to the limits but not beyond them. We experience "flow" not when we are doing something easy and routine, which requires little interest and generates little excitement, nor when we are doing something that is beyond our capacities and overwhelms us with complexities and demands. Rather we experience "flow" when we exercise the full vigor of our powers, when it is demanded of us that we do our

143

best. Csikszentmihalyi describes how chess, sports, mountain climbing, surgery can all be "flow" activities for those who are skilled in them. It is almost as though an "automatic pilot" takes over, and one does what one must do with a rich, full, enjoyment, reveling in the challenge and one's capacity to meet it.

I experience "flow" when I write, particularly when I know what I want to say, when I have command of the data and resources that I need, and when the whole article or book appears in my mind's eye laid out as a coherent, unified system. I need only to commit myself to the onflowing process of producing the book; the experience is neither dull nor overwhelming but challenging, satisfying. I can do what I am called on to do by the project, and I can do it with ease and skill (regardless of what the reviewers might say), but also with the full satisfaction that comes from knowing that one's abilities are being pushed to their limits.

It happens again for me on water skis (a safe and secure pair). Give me a strong motor, a fast boat, a good driver and a smooth lake and I can give myself over completely to the joyous rhythm of wind, air, water, and blades slicing across wakes. One plunges into the rhythm and is taken up by it, and without conscious thought or reflection, one weaves back and forth in a spontaneous, playful exercise of one's skills (which in my case happen to be moderate at best). Off to one side, back across the wake, off to the other side, weaving, spinning, turning, shifting the tow rope from hand to hand, not afraid of falling (foolishly, perhaps), but alert every second to the possibilities and challenges of the endlessly shifting environment of air and water in which one finds oneself. Muscles straining yet relaxed, wind beating fiercely but not painfully against the skin, one becomes unself-consciously part of the environment, bending with it, leaning on it, pitting one's resources against it, and enjoying every glorious second.

I also experience "flow" when sailing, especially in an offshore wind which produces a brisk and steady movement without high waves to endanger my fragile *Leprechaun*. Sailing for me is much like skiing, although it adds the extra dimension of the tension between sail, rope, and wind. I am not much of a sailor, but flow experiences need not require great skills; they only require situations which demand the best of the skills we have. One man's "flow" is another man's boredom and another's terror. If you are one of that rare breed who has climbed the Himalayas, then the small mountains in upstate New York will be boring. If you have never climbed a mountain at all, the upstate New York peaks might well be terrifying. And if you are a modest, beginning climber, wrestling the peak in New York to submission might be just within your capacities and can easily result in a "flow" experience for you.

Each of us can think of our own "flow" experiences. Tennis, golf, cooking, singing, working with power tools are some examples perhaps. My guess is that "flow" experiences, which abound in our daily lives, are the best concrete, practical anticipations we get of what the delights of the heavenly life might be.

It sounds like a pretty good deal....

There was someone who once said, "The kingdom of heaven is like a great banquet." And again he said, "The kingdom of heaven is like a marriage feast." What the hell (one should excuse the expression) is a great banquet or a marriage feast unless it's a crashing good party? There is a paradox, of course, in the notion of heaven/wedding banquet or heaven/party; but that is the nature of the parable style of Jesus. Sharp, contrasting pictures are pushed together to create surprise, wonder, tension. "Heaven" meant one kind of thing to his listeners and "party" meant something quite different. You put "heaven" and "party" together and you have limit-language, language which both records and triggers a limit-experience, which forces us to say, "Oh *that's* what he's talking about!"

Continued life, continued excitement, wonder, surprise, challenge, "flow," smashing great parties—those are the kinds of ordinary human experiences which best enable us, I think, to

145

anticipate what our continued life will be. We can, of course, spend too much time reflecting on it. The temptation to go back into my trance (an activity I am much better at, it turns out, than water-skiing) and investigate my marvelous mixture of Sherwood Forest, San Francisco, and Chicago is quite strong. But there are other things to be about. We prepare for the life that is to come not by fantasizing about it but by living hopefully, joyously, "flowing-ly," wonderfully in the present life. We prepare for the permanent resurrection festival by celebrating resurrection in the here and now. Each time we run the risk of dying to the old self so that we might rise to the new, we not only anticipate but we participate in that which is to come.

EASTER/RESURRECTION

E ASTER is the Christian spring festival. It asks a question as old as humankind. It does not even provide a new answer; there always has been a strong hunch in human nature that death does not say the final word. What the Christian spring feast adds is the power of its certainty that death is not ultimate. The resurrection of Jesus says to the Christian, and through him the rest of humankind, "Dream your most impossible dreams, fantasize your maddest fantasies, hope your wildest hopes, and when they all come to an end what the heavenly Father has prepared for you only begins, for eye has not seen nor has ear heard, nor has it entered into the heart of man what God has prepared for those who love him."

This may not be the way things really are. The data are inconclusive. Life may well be absurd, the universe random chance, existence without purpose. My point is that the resurrection of Jesus "symbolizes" for the Christian the unshakable conviction that the hope which is central in our personalities is correct; the resurrection is the revelation that it is all right to hope.

For many Christians this may seem to be a minimal statement of their faith, but I would suggest that it is the core of the faith from which everything else flows. What is harder to believe— that one man rose from the dead or that life triumphs over death for everyone? The resuscitation of one human is considered an extraordinary occurrence, but however marvelous it may be it is, after all, only one person. But the survival of life in its battle with death, the survival of the life of each one of us, despite death, is an astonishing, extraordinary, incredible, immense, overwhelming phenomenon. One can, with difficulty perhaps, accept the return to life of a single person, but the return to life of everyone? That is a staggering thought.

But that is what the resurrection means. It is important for a

147

Christian not merely or not even mainly because it tells of one man whose followers experienced him as alive after his death, but because it claims to imply the survival of everyone despite death.

It is much easier to waste time in endless arguments about the physical details of the resurrection of Jesus because we are not forced thereby to face the overwhelming challenge of what the resurrection purports to reveal to us about the nature of the universe, the relationship of God with man, and the meaning of human life.

The resurrection, then, did not occur to "prove" anything; it occurred—if it occurred at all—to tell us something. We argue about proofs because we do not want to have to face the challenge in what it tells us.

It is not easy to believe that we can trust our hopeful instincts. Some people who fancy themselves "modern" say that they simply cannot accept the resurrection of Jesus. If you believe in modern science, they say, then you have to write the resurrection off as beyond belief. Implicit in such a stance is the assumption that our superstitious ancestors—one step beyond howling savagery—found it easy to believe in the resurrection. Skepticism was not born with the advent of modern science. Belief in the resurrection and all the resurrection implies requires an immense leap of faith for everyone, be he sophisticated modern scientist or illiterate peasant. Belief in the resurrection means belief in one's own survival despite death, it means belief in the correctness of our own irradicable hopefulness. You don't need a Ph.D. in science to find it hard to be hopeful. There is ugliness, suffering, and misery in the universe; life frequently seems to be a ghastly joke, and human events seem often enough to be under the control of a cruel and vicious fate. Though the data are inconclusive, they often seem to "tilt" toward despair.

The spring message, reinforced and revalidated by the story of Jesus, seems hopelessly naive: Life is not the ultimate reality, death is. Birth is the beginning of a brief and futile struggle between two oblivions. Our predecessors were just as likely to form such conclusions as modern, scientifically trained contemporaries. But there is still the miracle of spring, still laughter, still joy, still celebration, still hope. Hints, signals, "rumors"—try as we might to erase them, our hope persists in their existence. The story that Jesus was dead and now lives is believed by Christians as a validation of that hope.

It is a mistake to think, as many Christians seem to, that Jesus was an actor playing a part. They would believe that he went up to Jerusalem knowing that he was going to die with a precise and clear notion of how the heavenly Father was going to validate his preaching. He went through the act, played his part, saw the drama to its end. There was a day or two of anxiety, perhaps, a few hours of acute suffering, and then triumph.

One could admire the acting skill of someone who played such a role, though one could hardly identify with him, because we all go to our own deaths full of fear, hesitancy, and uncertainty. We may be confident that death is not the end, but we are still terrified at the prospect. If we read the New Testament carefully, we see that this was the case for Jesus too. He knew that the heavenly Father would confirm his preaching. He knew it with a greater and a different kind of knowledge than the rest of us possess, but he was not an actor playing a part; he was a human who shared the terror that we all have when faced with death.

It is the Christian conviction that Jesus is the Word of God. By this the Christian means that God speaks to us through the life and death and the new life of Jesus in a special and unique way. He speaks to us, of course, in all of His creation, particularly through our fellow humans. But Jesus, while he was human like us, was also someone "special" (and the greatest problem of Christianity is to explain the nature of that specialness). Jesus was special precisely because God's Word was spoken through him. In the life, the death, and new life of Jesus, God reveals to us what human existence is all about. In a way, one might even say that God "cheats," for Jesus represents an intervention in human events that was not "preprogrammed"' it was something extraordinarily unique, a special revelation that did not have to be, a revelation designed to confirm our wildest hopes.

Let it be clear, then, what Easter means to Christians. It is not a denial of death, it is not a pollyanna pretense that there is no suffering or ugliness or tragedy or absurdity in the universe. Easter represents the Christian acceptance of the fact of death in all its ugliness. It represents the Christian's assertion that there is evil aplenty in the world, but nature is reborn in the springtime, the sun rises every morning, we are reborn every time we experience a decisive personality growth. So the Christian believes through the revelation in the resurrection of Jesus that death does not have the final word and that evil will not have the final victory. Easter morning conveys a very simple message: Life is *almost* a complete and tragic disaster but not quite. At the very last second, the tragedy of human life is turned into comedy, and the existence of the human personality and the human race has a happy ending.

Chapter Seven

———————

Love: The Essence of Christianity

THE JOY OF LOVE

HILAIRE BELLOC, the English Catholic writer, in one of his "Cautionary Verses," announces: "Wherever the Catholic sun does shine/there is music and laughter and good red wine/At least I've found it so./Benedicamus Domino." Belloc was unquestionably comparing the festivity of his beloved Catholic Mediterranean culture with the moroseness of some northern European puritanical versions of Protestantism. By those standards, heaven knows, we Catholics are indeed a festive crowd. Yet we are hardly immune from the curse of sour-faced saints. Many of our non-Catholic and non-Christian neighbors and friends would scarcely describe us as easy-going, celebratory, joyous humans. On the contrary, we are often grim, somber and dour, preoccupied with sin, damnation and guilt, solemnly insisting on obedience to the letter of multitudinous rules and laws and so uptight about our faith as to be unable to relax or enjoy ourselves. Those who are attracted to Catholic Christianity and eventually become Catholics rarely mention that the principal appeal is the joyfulness of the Catholics they know. Music, laughter, good red wine? Not so's you'd notice it, unfortunately.

Note the kind of instructions Jesus gives the first ones who are going forth to be associates and colleagues. It would be a mistake to read that gospel passage as merely advice about logistical or financial arrangements. The point is not that the followers of Jesus traveled light; and the lesson for us is not necessarily a vow of poverty. The point is that Jesus' followers were carefree, and the lesson for us is one of joy.

If Christianity has not spread to the ultimate corners of the earth, if many people find its Catholic version to be singularly unattractive, the fault does not reside either in the gospel or in the Catholic Christian heritage, but in Catholic Christians who have not been joyous enough, nor hopeful enough, nor merry enough, nor carefree enough. There is much talk about "evangelization" in the church today, and that is all to the good. The church is in the evangelization business. But sometimes people seem to confuse evangelization with high pressure, mass media publicity or with organizational membership drives, or with "convert-making" techniques. There may not be anything wrong with methods, drives, techniques, and gimmicks (though on occasion there may be), but it is important that every Catholic Christian understand that the essence of evangelization is not a technique, a gimmick, a drive, or a plan; the essence of evangelization is joyous, carefree, happy love. An evangelization campaign which is not animated by such carefree love and not staffed by joyous, happy Christians will simply not work. Indeed, it may very well do more harm than good.

The love must not be forced, must not be phony, must not be the smothering, sticky, sweet love of some religious enthusiasts who oppress other people by their love or by what they pretend is love when it is in fact merely skillful manipulation. It must be *real* love, the kind of love that leaves other human beings free to make their own choices, just as it was quite clear to Jesus' followers that they were to constrain or to compel no one to embrace the gospel. It was a free option to be lovingly offered and lovingly accepted without any constraint, even the constraint that may masquerade as loving affection. We cannot approach other human beings with the pretense of knowing the answers to what life really means if we do not, by the kind of lives we live, demonstrate that our faith does put meaning in our life and makes us more generously loving, more humane, more compassionate and free within our own self-possession and our relationship to others. We cannot short-circuit the process, we cannot substitute high-pressure, sophisticated gimmickry and the hard sell for the witness of a free, mature, generous, loving life.

It might be argued that we Catholic Christians have a long way to go before we even begin to approach the ideal of joy expressed

154

in "laughter and music and good red wine." Nor would very many people view us as carefree followers of Jesus of the sort described in the gospel. We cannot delay the preaching of the gospel until we become saints ourselves, of course; it would never happen. But we should at least be clear in our own minds as to the kind of lives we ought to live so that our preaching of the gospel will be something more than a mindless bleating of words in an empty hall.

How does one become carefree? Perhaps more to the point, why should one be carefree? Are there not enough cares and worries in the world to keep us mired indefinitely? Is it not false to be joyous? Should we not be somber and serious because that is precisely the appropriate response to the mess the world is in? Is not the sour-faced saint in fact the good Christian? Is not his or her sour face reflecting the disastrous state of the human condition and God's legitimate anger over all the sin in the world? What is there to be all that hopeful about? That question, of course, brings us to the essence of Christianity, a religion whose center is good news. Indeed, the good news is that God's forgiving, reconciling, saving love is far stronger than all the evil, all the tragedy, all the suffering in the world. Even death ultimately yields to the power of God's love. It is just that simple. We believe it, then necessarily we live lives of joy and hopefulness. We will then be truly fundamentally carefree, no matter how many cares there might be in our lives.

FOLLOW YOUR INSTINCTS

ONE of the toughest things in life is making decisions—where to go to school, what kind of a job to get, who to marry, where to live, whether to move, whether to change jobs. All of these things require an aye or nay; we cannot stay home *and* go away; we cannot go south *and* north too. Indeed, the more complicated our lives get the more decisions we have to make, and each generation seems to have even more decisions to face than its predecessors.

Decision-making is difficult precisely because we can never be certain about the outcome. We can calculate the odds, estimate the probabilities, gather computer print-outs to tell us what our chances are; but in the final analysis every decision requires some kind of risks. If there were no risks, there would be no need for a decision. Some of us try to hedge, try to get through life without making decisions, responding always to external pressures by yielding to whichever are the strongest. The nice thing about that strategy is that we can always blame some force outside ourselves when we've made a mistake. The bad thing about it is that we then lead lives devoid of personal responsiblity.

Life requires many leaps in the dark, many acts of almost blind trust, many risks that have been calculated carefully but are still risky. Following our instincts, "playing it by ear," is part of the human condition whether we like it or not. Still there are times when we *know* that however uncertain the odds, however imponderable the eventuality, however unpredictable the outcome, we simply know that there is something we should do—go to this school, choose that career, marry this person. We do not ignore rational calculations but go beyond their limits and take the leap of faith, a leap which seems blind but which we know in our hearts is the leap to take.

We must very carefully understand what happens in such decisive acts. We may say that we "feel" what we should do, or that our "instincts" tell us what we should do, that we have a "hunch" that it will work out all right. In fact, what we usually mean is that we are using certain styles of knowing that go beyond rationality and combine all the resources of personality—instincts, emotion, will, subconscious and unconscious. They all combine to tell us that this particular decision responds to that which is best, most generous, most outgoing, and most authentic in ourselves. Marry this man or woman? The odds are that it would be a good thing, but in the depths of our personality we also *know* beyond any calculation that this is indeed a person we should marry.

It is precisely to that sharp, refined, deep part of our personality that the Holy Spirit speaks. Paul tells us that God's Spirit speaks to our spirit. He means that the Paraclete, the one who Jesus promised in this gospel is God inviting, calling forth that which is most noble, most authentic, most appealing, most generous in us. It is to our "hunch," "instinct," and "feel" that the Spirit appeals; he does not deny rationality, of course, and he assumes that rationality is at work. The Paraclete goes beyond rationality, however, and appeals to that which is most authentic in the total human person that is each one of us. God's Spirit, in other words, usually works on us quite indirectly, speaking to us, appealing to us, inviting us, calling us forth in and through the people and opportunities that daily come our way.

The Paraclete, then, does not come down and whisper in our ear—though sometimes the power of his call is so strong that it is almost as though there is a voice telling us what to do. We *know* which decision is most authentically us, and we know, if we stop to think about it, that the Spirit is calling.

Our instincts can be wrong, of course, our hunches inaccurate, our "feel" self-deceptive. This supra-irrational way of knowing is by no means infallible. We may think the Paraclete is inviting us when in fact it is a "false" Spirit (which does not necessarily or ordinarily imply demonic activity—it only implies a mistake).

157

One of the reasons for having a community of friends—we call it the church—is that it can help us discern the Spirit and help us distinguish between the true and false spirits. That community can listen with us; and, knowing us better sometimes than we know ourselves, our friends can tell us, "You know, you're really kidding yourself," or, "Yeah, that does seem to be the right thing for you." And internally in our personalities, the Paraclete is a Spirit of peace. It is not the peace of absolute tranquility but that of challenge and excitement. If that to which we seem to be called by the Paraclete brings us greater peace with ourselves, our family, and our friends, makes us more open and loving and generous to those with whom we come in contact, then it is very likely the true Paraclete and not the false Spirit who is talking to us.

Christians have known for a long time that the Spirit speaks to us through others, going above and beyond the ordinary calculations of rationality. For centuries our predecessors evolved "rules" that showed remarkable insight into the human psychology and the human propensity for self-deception. In our era we seem to have lost a sense of the Holy Spirit and understanding of the need to discern the operations of the Paraclete. Very recently, however, we have become much more aware of the Spirit's work in the world in and through other human beings. It is therefore time for each one of us to review the operations of this secret depth or leading edge of our personality, to understand how it has worked in our life, to come to terms with its weakness and its strength, and to learn from our own mistakes so that in the future, when we are "playing it by ear," we may be able to tell whether what we are hearing is a false spirit or the Paraclete who has come to teach us all truth.

THE LORD IS AT HAND

PAROUSIA will come suddenly. Our own death will come suddenly. But even more important is the fact that Jesus has already come suddenly, and that in him God intervened dramatically in human history. Now is the eschatological hour; the crisis is present today; the opportunities are at hand. The important sudden event will not happen sometime in the future; it happens today in the lives we are living. Jesus is present most critically for us at this very moment.

It is a triumphant, victorious procession that wends its way up to Zion to celebrate the eschatological age; and with that same spirit of joy and anticipation, Paul announces that the darkness of night is to be put off and the armor of light is at hand. There is a warning in the gospel message, but it is a warning issued in the context of joy. The Lord is at hand. Christian hope, while it certainly has a reference to the future, is fundamentally focused in the present. The Christian expects life and happiness in the future precisely because he knows God loves him *now*, because Jesus is present in his life *now* bearing witness to God's saving love. Unlike the Marxist or some of our contemporary non-Marxist worshippers of the future, the Christian does not root his expectations in future events; he does not ground his hopes in the dawning of a new day; he does not think that the eschatological age is beginning with the advent of Consciousness III. For the Christian, these marvelous events have already happened and are occurring even now. The eschatological day is not about to dawn; it has dawned already. Consciousness III was not born on the campus of Yale University but in Jerusalem. The Christian hopes not in a future to come but in a future already here.

The Christian, then, does not say that things are going to get better someday; he says things are better already because we know through Jesus how much God loves us. The great events have happened and are happening. The Son of Man will indeed return to fulfill his work, but more important than his eventual return is the fact that he came and the fact that he still comes. The Christian is, of course, confident about the future, but he cares less about the future than about seizing the glorious opportunities of the present moment.

We all know what it is like for our lives to change suddenly. One day everything is right. Our friends smile at us, our family is affectionate, our boss is pleased with our work, our food is good, the news on the TV is not as bad as usual, our life goes on optimistically, the future looks right. Then the weather turns bad, we come down with a cold, our spouse is moody, our children rambunctious, our coworkers surly, the car won't start, we get a headache, there's a terrible traffic jam, we get a bill we had forgotten about, and the telephone rings just after we get to sleep at night. The day never should have started.

This rhythmic periodicity of life is so normal that we take it for granted. And anyone who resents such a rhythm of ups and downs is being childish. But what really shocks us is the eruption of sudden, tragic news in times of happiness. We read about a groom dying on a honeymoon, a man being killed just after getting a new job, someone coming home safe from Vietnam only to be killed in an alley. When the ups and downs of life become dramatic and traumatic we become quite conscious that there is a titantic struggle between good and evil in the world, and evil often seems to win.

Jesus never doubted the reality of this struggle. He who was with God in a unique, special way was also man. He had become man precisely to engage in the battle between good and evil, to tilt the scales in favor of goodness, to assure mankind that in the long run the forces of terror, entrapment, destruction and death would be routed, that humans were indeed free to trust and love one another. Palm Sunday represented the height of his success, the pinnacle of his triumph as a prophet. He was indeed hailed as a messenger from God who had brought good news of life and love. But his triumph was to end in tragedy. His "good day" on that Sunday was to turn into a "bad day" on the following Friday. Everything that went "right" on Sunday would go "wrong" less than a week later. Goodness triumphed in the hosannas of Palm Sunday; evil would counterattack on Friday and apparently win a decisive victory.

But it all had to be this way. Jesus had to share in the painful and poignant ambiguity of the human condition; he had to enjoy the heights of human triumph and endure the depths of human suffering so that Easter would not appear as an easy and cheap victory, but a triumph earned at the price of great effort and sacrifice. We do not know why good and evil, triumph and tragedy, joy and suffering are intermingled so intimately in our confusing world. The Cross and Resurrection do not finally answer that mystery. But we do learn two critical things: (1) Good does triumph over evil—finally and decisively. (2) The triumph is not an easy one but must be earned at a terrible cost.

WHEN TIME STANDS STILL

THERE are occasions in the life of each of us when time stands still, when the whole world seems to rush in upon us benignly and graciously, when we find ourselves caught up in emotions of great peace and joy, when we see the unity of everything in the universe, when warmth and happiness seem to fill us to the brim and overflow. These brief interludes of peace and joy may be almost unbearably powerful or they may be very light and gentle; they may be a deep "mystical" experience or merely a pleasant, quiet interlude that catches us unawares. These transient episodes, which usually just "happen," show us hints of what life is all about; but it doesn't last, and even while we reach out to hold it tighter, the brief moment, when our lives and everything that has happened to us seem to make sense, recedes.

The transfiguration of Jesus was an overwhelmingly powerful version of those little interludes of peace and joy we all experience in our lives, those transient interludes when we see exactly what our lives are all about and what we must do if we are to be true to ourselves. For most of us these "religious experiences" are not very powerful and do not give dominant tone and direction to our lives, though for some people (perhaps a quarter of the population), according to recent statistics, these experiences are very powerful and very important. For most of us they are merely a hint of an explanation, but for some they are a road map with the path marked out from which they are unable to deviate.

Such was the experience of Jesus in the transfiguration. His public life was drawing to a close, he knew he had done just about all he could to preach the Good News of his heavenly Father's Kingdom. Now something else awaited him to finish his mission, but as far as human knowledge was concerned it was not yet fully clear what had to be done. On Mount Tabor, in the midst of the overwhelmingly powerful transfiguration experience, it became clear to Jesus what he had to do. He had to go up to Jerusalem and suffer and die for the Kingdom he was preaching. The Tabor experience was one of joy and glory, but it was also an overwhelmingly powerful command to Jesus. He must go up to Jerusalem and die.

For the early Christians the circle was complete. In his moment of glory, Jesus saw that he must die, but his death in its turn would produce the final glory of the resurrection. The transfiguration was both the anticipation of Easter and the command to go forward to Good Friday. Mark, arguing as he does throughout his gospel against those who wish to turn Jesus into nothing more than a worker of marvels, strongly emphasizes that the glory of the transfiguration experience should be kept secret until after the death and resurrection of Jesus. One could only understand Tabor, in other words, in light of Calvary, because Calvary links Tabor to Easter. Jesus had to come down from the mountain, enter the depths of human suffering in order that he might finally rise up.

There is a profound psychological and human truth in this insight. We must suffer before we can exult. In the ordinary experiences of growth in our daily lives, we only become better human beings by dying to a part of ourselves. The close relationship between a husband and wife, for example, can only expand and grow into a deeper and richer love if man and woman are willing to die to their selfish defensive, punitive, vindictive, impatient inclinations. Marriage begins with a transfiguration experience. A married couple go down into a valley of suffering together before they can come up on the other side and experience even greater joy than at the beginning of their marriage. This cycle of joy and suffering and then greater joy goes on frequently, sometimes even daily, in their life together.

So it is with us. Our lives offer us frequent interludes of joy—little Tabors if not big ones—and in these interludes we catch hints of the great joy that seems to be beckoning us and calling to us. But then the interlude passes and the monotony, the heartache,

163

the routine and the anxieties of life return. We must ask ourselves whether the interludes of joy or the interludes of sorrow are the better hint of what life is all about. There is no way any of us can escape suffering in this life; the issue is whether we bear it bravely as an interlude and even a cause of our subsequent joy, or whether we rebel against it and try to avoid entering the valley of sorrow. Eventually we all enter that valley; we all die. The question is *how* will we die?

The research of Elisabeth Kubler-Ross on those who are resuscitated after "death" would indicate that all experience transfiguration-like episodes as the moment of death. Some resent being pulled back into life, and none of them, she tells us, are ever afraid to die again. Dr. Kubler-Ross says that she is convinced now, as a matter of scientific certainty, that death does not end life. This certainly follows the parallel path of the Christian conviction that life and death and more life are inextricably related. As the poet Francis Thompson says: "Death and birth are inseparable upon the earth, for they are twain yet one, and death is birth."

BREAK BREAD TOGETHER

ONE of the most painful things in the world is to eat alone; one of the most enjoyable things in the world is eating with our friends. If we want to understand what human loneliness is, we have only to go to one of those big city cafeterias where one can always find at least a score of people sitting by themselves eating in silence. Since it just doesn't seem natural not to have someone to talk to, someone to share with as we eat our meal, we feel profoundly sorry for those poor lonely men and women who must eat all their meals by themselves. Somehow they seem cut off from the rest of the human race. The message of the Eucharist is that we need never eat alone. Oh, occasionally, and perhaps even frequently, we may have to take our meals by ourselves, but we are never really alone because Jesus is with us. Jesus who fed the multitudes, Jesus who enjoyed the table fellowship of his apostles is the very same Jesus who is with us not merely in the meal of Mass but wherever we are and wherever we go. No matter how alone or cut off we may feel, Jesus shares the table with us. The Mass means that Jesus has come to eliminate loneliness from human life. Even though we may occasionally be alone, as long as we believe in the love which Jesus manifested when he fed the multitudes, we know that there is no reason for us to be lonely.

Many modern scripture commentators tell us that while the Last Supper was indeed the last meal that Jesus ate with his followers before his execution, it was not by any means the first of the "table fellowships" which Jesus shared with his disciples. Eating a meal together had deeply religious significance for all small religious groups in the time of Jesus. Therefore, it is very likely that the table fellowships which Jesus shared with his apostles before the Last Supper were religious meals in tone and symbolism. The Mass is, of course, many things: a sacrifice, a sacrament, a memorial.

165

But above all else, the Mass is a meal and it plays its role as a sacrifice, a sacrament, and a memorial precisely insofar as it is a banquet. However, the Mass is not just an ordinary banquet; it is a wedding banquet, a meal celebrating a love that flames among people who are deeply in love with one another. This may sound both surprising and shocking to us. Mass rarely looks like a wedding banquet—frequently it doesn't look like any kind of meal at all—and we are just a little bit dismayed to hear it said of something as sacred as the Mass that it celebrates a passionate love affair. But we should not be dismayed, for Jesus has compared the kingdom of his heavenly father to a wedding banquet and the Mass is a union between Jesus and his followers in that kingdom. Furthermore, Paul compares the love between Jesus and his church to the love between a man and a woman. The Mass is a celebration of the union between Jesus and his church; therefore, to say that the Mass is a celebration of a passionate love does not seem to be an exaggeration. We sing and celebrate at Mass because we are convinced that God is deeply in love with us.

Those of us who assemble around the altar to eat the bread of the Eucharist necessarily and inevitably commit ourselves to do all we can to eliminate physical suffering in the world. Hunger, poverty, ignorance, sickness, misery—none of these have any place in the world in which the eucharistic banquet is celebrated. We are under no illusion that they can be eliminated immediately; nonetheless, as Christians we must consider ourselves committed to do all in our power to overcome physical suffering. Just as Jesus did, we must take compassion on the multitudes, even if we realize our compassion is not going to be completely effective. The war on poverty began not in Washington in the early 1960s but along the shore of the sea at Tiberias nineteen centuries ago. Anyone who is not committed to that war is not a Christian; anyone who is not deeply committed to it cannot eat the eucharistic bread with an easy conscience. This is not to say that there is any specific way of "feeding the hungry" which every Christian must follow;

much less to say that specific legislation is endorsed by the gospel. But it is to say that every Christian must be profoundly concerned about hunger—or any other kind of human misery—wherever it occurs, and he must do all that he can to work for its elimination.

One need not at all intend to minimize the importance of the theological controversies that are raised over the Eucharist by saying that there is a danger that our concern about these controversies may blind us to the basic message of the eucharistic banquet. The exact explanation of how Jesus is present is not nearly as important as the fact that the Eucharist is a communion with Jesus and his work. It *does* bring those who eat of it into contact with a new life, a life which is the "springtime of the world." It *does* make them an integral part of the great historical process which began on Sinai and was renewed in the Upper Room. It *does* give them a share in the sacrifice and suffering of Jesus and it *does* promise them ultimate reunion with Jesus in the new life of the Resurrection. Neither the theological discussions which have gone on through the centuries, nor the exegetical considerations described in previous paragraphs should cause us to overlook the message of Mark's gospel: *He who eats with the bread of the Eucharist is really in communion with Jesus and is working together with him in fulfilling his covenant.*

Nor should we overlook the essentially *familial* nature of the eucharistic event. Whether it actually was the day of the Passover or not is less important than the fact that it was a family banquet, that is to say, a small intimate gathering of a group of close friends. The early Christians, whatever their understanding of the precise relationship between the Lord's Supper and the Passover, were quite aware that the Lord's Supper was a gathering of people who loved one another. In other words, the covenant of Jesus was a covenant rooted in a love feast of a group of intimate friends. To the extent that eucharistic banquets do not manifest this profound affection which Jesus and his apostles felt for one another, they are less than adequate symbols of what the Eucharist really means.

We may not always know the person next to us in church, and that is perhaps a misfortune, but if we are not prepared to love that person who is next to us, or anyone else who is in the church, then we simply do not understand what the Eucharist means—no matter how sophisticated our theology or our exegesis may be.

We know that man does hunger after meaning and purpose and faith. We know that satisfaction that comes from having to cope with physical hunger. We can even understand how the Good News of Jesus can protect us from ever being spiritually hungry again. The purpose and the meaning the Good News puts into our life makes it impossible for us to drift into chaos and confusion. It is not merely a banquet of wisdom as described in the first reading from the Book of Proverbs. It is a kind of unity with God and his Messenger for which there was no preparation in the Old Testament. So intimate is the union that it could be described as actually taking the flesh and blood of Jesus physically into our bodies in such a way that we would, as Paul says in the epistle, be drugged, not with wine but with the spirit—so drugged, in fact, we would sing and chant, "The true Lord." It is obvious that Jesus is speaking of a form of union with God that is quite new, although many ancient religions did have sacrificial banquets in which some sort of unity with the deity was established by eating the sacrificial victim. The Eucharist represents the most intimate union that is possible between Jesus and us and between God and us through Jesus. The love of Jesus for his followers was such that he would remain somehow or other present with them through the Eucharist, bringing life now not only through his teaching but by his presence.

OUR FATHER

A DOLESCENCE, it is said, is a time when a young man believes that he will never become as dumb as his father is. If such an epigram is correct, then presumably adulthood is the time when one discovers that one's father has learned a lot in the last several years and is now not so dumb after all. Childhood is the time when one thinks one's parents know everything and can do everything. Disillusionment about parents is part of growing from childhood to adolescence; rediscovery of parents is part of growing from adolescence to adulthood. The theme of Luke's gospel is that the authentic Christian adult is one who lives with childlike trust in the heavenly Father. You become a Christian adult when you rediscover, or discover for the first time, that you can *really* trust God.

People who have carefully studied the scripture agree that the passage we hear in this gospel is one of the most important sections in all of the scripture. It is important not merely because it provides us with one version of the prayer we say every day (a shorter version, you will notice—think of how much time you could save if you said the shorter "Our Father" instead of the longer one!), but because it is the best and clearest evidence we have of the relationship Jesus claimed to have with his Father in heaven.

Most religions of the world and most religious leaders have spoken of God as "the Father," but the English translation, "Father," does not begin to convey what the Hebrew word *Abba* really means. It is not a formal, respectful title of honor; it's a casual, informal, affectionate word that a little child might use toward an indulgent father who is bouncing him or her on his knee. *Abba* could better be translated, "Pop" or "Daddy" or "Daddy-o." Adults in the time of Jesus used the term of their earthly fathers, but only in intimate conversations and only at very special times.

169

There is no record anywhere in all Hebraic literature—scripture or otherwise—of anyone ever being so bold, so presumptuous, so disrespectful as to call the Father in heaven by the affectionate term *Abba*. Those who heard Jesus use it must have been profoundly shocked, and the early Christians were also uneasy with the word, because when they translated it into Latin and Greek they used two much more solemn and respectful words. Who did Jesus think he was, daring to call the Lord of creation, the Alpha and the Omega, the Prime Mover, Being itself, the Ground of Being, by a name very much like "Pops" or, as the Irish would say, the "Ould Fella"?

The answer is that Jesus presumed to address the heavenly Father so familiarly because he claimed a special relationship of intimacy with him, a relationship absolutely different, unique, and totally unheard of ever before in human history. Virtually all of our Christology, all of our thinking about the presence of divinity in Jesus can ultimately be traced to and grounded in this claim of special, affectionate relationship with the Father in heaven. But Jesus was not claiming such a relationship in order to exalt his own role or to find arguments for the theology books of the future. He was more interested in revealing something about God than in defining his own role. In calling God "Abba," he was saying in effect that the Ultimate is the sort of Being with whom one can enter friendly, intimate, casual, informal, relaxed, lovingly affectionate relationships. The Ground of Being, in other words, is a Thou.

More than that, Jesus told us that we too, can call him "Daddy-o" or "the Ould Fella" if we want. It is not blasphemous, not irreverent, not insulting; it's the kind of lovingly affectionate relationship that the heavenly Father wants. For Jesus, in teaching his followers the Lord's Prayer, told them that they, too, could dare to call the heavenly Father by the name "Abba;" they, too, could claim a relationship of affectionate intimacy with the maker of everyone and everything. Again, it was a profoundly shock-

170

ing, a terribly scandalous, an outrageous suggestion. Christians have backed away from it ever since Jesus first taught the Lord's Prayer. It just doesn't seem right to think about God or to talk about him that way—not even if he himself insisted, through Jesus, that it is all right to do so. We know, in other words, what God wants better than God does!

The other side of the coin is that if we can be so lovingly affectionate with God, then we are justified in having the same trust in him that a child has in the father he calls "Da-da" or the mother he calls "Ma-ma." When we grow older we discover that our human mothers and fathers do not know everything and cannot do everything; they have their faults, limitations, imperfections just like everyone else. Still we have pleasant memories of the time when our mother and father were our whole world and we believed that nothing was impossible for them. They could make every hurt go away, they could gratify every need, they could respond to every love. Psychological adulthood requires us to realize that our parents are not omniscient, omnipotent; but religious adulthood, for the Christian at any rate, requires that we become so mature, so sophisticated, so brave that we can commit ourselves to trust and love and affection to our heavenly Father who does know everything and can do everything. He cares for us the way a doting father does for a little kid in his arms. It is a very brave and very wise person who can live that way.

How many times have we said the "Our Father" during our life? Do we really live like we believe that the Father in heaven can provide our daily bread and everything else we need? In the power of his affectionate love, are we really strong enough to forgive those who have offended us? Are we really ready to live lives of love and trust, affection and forgiveness?

KING ON A DONKEY

IN T.S. Eliot's words, "The last temptation is the greatest treason: to do the right deed for the wrong reason." The crowds of citizens of Jerusalem who hailed Jesus very properly hailed a Messiah and a King but they hailed him for the wrong reason—the wrong reason is interpreted by the Synoptics as political power; by John as a narrow nationalism. But we should criticize the citizens of Jerusalem only when we are certain that we ourselves are not distorting the message of Jesus to serve our own purpose and our own self-seeking and nationalistic goals. So often we use the good news that Jesus has brought to us to justify ourselves and to condemn others; to sit in judgment on those whose manners or attitudes or values are different from ours. The identification of Christianity with the goals of an individual, tribe, neighborhood, city or nation did not stop when Jesus entered Jerusalem but continues even to our day. The triumphalistic interpretation of the kingship of Jesus which justifies our own prejudices is inconsistent with the King sitting humbly on the donkey and coming to gather the oppressed around him.

Do those of us who are young have room to listen to the wisdom of the old; and do those of us who are older have the restraint necessary to learn from the young? Can those of us who are white listen patiently to the protests of the blacks, and understand why human beings are forced to protest? And can those of us who are black understand the fears and the anxieties that these protests bring to those of us who are white? Can those of us who are men be sympathetic and compassionate enough to be able to see things from the viewpoint of our women? Can those of us who are women be tolerant and patient enough to understand why men may see things differently from women? The young who will not attempt to understand the old; the old who will not be sympathetic to the young; the white who will not seek justice for the black; the black who feels justified in hating the white; the man who is unthinking to women; and the woman who manipulates her man all belong in the crowd at the gates of Jerusalem for they have all missed the point of Jesus' message, and have completely overlooked the symbolism of the King on the donkey, and the reflection of that symbolism in Paul's maxim: "Neither male nor female, Greek nor Roman, Jew nor Gentile, but all one in Christ Jesus."

THE GRATUITY OF LOVE

IN ONE of D. H. Lawrence's short stories a young doctor walking through the countryside observes a girl, apparently in a trance, walk into a pool and quickly sink over her head. She is a morose, rather unfriendly person whose brothers are friends of the young man. The whole family is about to leave that part of the country because of financial setbacks. Without a second thought he dashes down to the pond, wades in over his head and pulls out the now unconscious girl. He carries her to his home and revives her. The girl is so overwhelmed by the discovery that he has risked his life to save hers that she becomes convinced that he must love her. Her passion is contagious and the young doctor discovers that indeed he has begun to love her. Frightened of what she says, the girl tries to draw off from the commitment; but the young doctor, now thoroughly in love, will not listen to her. He loves her and that is that.

The short story "The Horsetrader's Daughter" has exactly the same theme as the parable of the shepherd who risks the rest of his flock to pursue one lost sheep. It's a bizarre, absurd, foolish investment of time and energy that can in no way be justified by the cost. Similarly, in another parable, to neglect nine silver pieces for the pursuit of one piece is an absurd risk. You are probably not going to find the lost piece and in the meantime you could easily lose the other nine. Finally, having found the one lost piece of silver your neighbors are going to think that you are utterly crazy when you call them in to celebrate the fact you've finally found a lost fifty-cent piece. The point of the parable, however, is that God's behavior, judged by human standards, is crazy. God's love, like all real love, does not count the cost, does not act rationally, does not behave sensibly.

The young doctor in D. H. Lawrence's story had never found the woman attractive. His impulse to prevent her suicide was sud-

174

den and unreflective. Falling in love with her as he held her soggy, battered little body in his arms was lunacy. When her brothers found out they would certainly laugh at him, and the people in his district would be baffled as to why a promising young practitioner should fall in love with such an odd girl. His affection for her was as crazy as that of the shepherd pursuing the worthless sheep, the woman hunting for the trivial coin, the father of the prodigal son going down the road to greet that returning wastrel. But that's the way love is; it hedges no bets, counts no costs, computes no formulae, calculates no interest rates; it simply loves and that is that.

Is not Jesus inconsistent? One time he advises us to calculate very carefully what we're getting into before we follow him. Another time he tells us that love does not calculate but rather is absurd and irrational, lunatic and half-mad. Why the apparent contradiction? In fact, first Jesus was talking about us and later talking about the heavenly Father. Given our own weaknesses and frailties, he warns that we had better calculate carefully before we respond to the absurd, whimsical, half-mad love of God for us—at least half-mad by our own human standards of calculation. God has no more ''business'' falling in love with us than the shepherd has going off hunting for the lost sheep, or than D. H. Lawrence's doctor had falling in love with the strange, moody horsetrader's daughter. God does it just the same.

There is something wildly reckless about the God that is portrayed in these parables of mercy. He has parties over foolish things to celebrate unimportant events. He showers good things on sinners before they can even adequately express their compunction. He engages in foolish and frantic searches which, if we were to undertake them, would make us an object of ridicule. There is something just a little bit berserk about this God of ours. As a matter of fact, this bizarre behavior of his is almost embarrassing to us. Surely Jesus must be engaging in some kind of oriental, rhetorical exaggeration. He cannot expect us to believe that God literally rejoices over each individual one of us no matter how worthless we may be.

However, we must remember that the reality of God's love for us is *underestimated* by the story of the crazy shepherd or the foolish woman celebrating the discovery of a lost half-dollar. By human standards, God's love is even wilder, more unfathomable, more absurd than the fixation of the shepherd on the single sheep or the woman on the lost coin or the young doctor on the pathetic girl. To say that God is fixated on us is not to exaggerate but rather to speak something less than the full, rich truth.

MOTHER'S LOVE

DURING his all-too-brief September pastorate, Pope John Paul I said one day in a talk that the love of God was more like the love of a mother than the love of a father. There was horror and shock in many of the Italian newspapers. A number of writers were eager to explain that either there was no basic change in Christian doctrine or that there had been a basic change and that now there was a fourth person in the Blessed Trinity. In his next public homily the "smiling pope" laughed it all off by saying that he was only quoting the prophet Isaiah.

It may have been that Pope John Paul I was only repeating traditional doctrine. Nevertheless, the way he said it and the occasion on which he said it, in a simple public audience, was both shattering and effective. As William and Nancy McCready put it in an article several years ago, God is a mother, father, brother, sister, lover, friend. Every human love we know is but a reflection of God's love. Pope John Paul I who, it would seem, had a superb relationship with his mother, spoke of the maternal love of God, emphasizing thereby the maternal, affectionate, nurturing, supportive, binding-up-the-cut-finger-with-a-band-aid dimension of God's love. In a Catholic Christian religious tradition, the essential role of the Blessed Mother has been to manifest and reveal the maternal side of God. It is appropriate, to reflect on Mary, the "sacrament" (that is to say, the *revealing symbol*) of God's maternal love. God does indeed care for us the way a mother cares for a little baby, the way Mary cared for Jesus in Nazareth and Bethlehem. Despite all our fears, our failures, and our anxieties, we still believe in that tender, maternal side of God's love, in a smile something like that of Pope John Paul I.

What do mothers do? They comfort you when you are sick, provide food, answer questions, take good care of you, and, more important than anything else, make sure that you know you're loved. Sometimes they are impatient, angry, sometimes they repri-

177

mand you or even punish you. But still, your mother is the woman who has carried you in her body for nine months, brought you into the world, protected you when you were a helpless infant, and the person who loves you more than anyone else in the world— at least in our culture where it is the mother who can most afford to show her affection for you. At best, mother's love is gentle, kind, tender, reassuring, comforting, free. That is the way Mary loved Jesus, that is the way God loves us.

It often doesn't seem that way. Each of us looks back and sees disappointment, heartache, failure, tragedy. If God loves us so much why does he permit these things to happen? Why did he permit John Paul I to die so soon? Why does he permit anyone to die? It is a strange kind of mother's love when God claims to love us as a mother and then lets us suffer and die. The answer we can give is that a little baby does not understand why its mother permits it to cry and suffer even though she assures the baby it is temporary and may even be for his or her own good, so we can never hope to understand God's designs for us. Indeed, the difference between a baby's intelligence and the mother's intelligence is minor compared to the difference between our intelligence and God's. It is the most difficult part of our faith to accept that a loving, maternal God can permit such apparently terrible tragedies. Though we are nonetheless committed to our faith, the joy that will come eventually will be so enormous that we will forget the suffering just as the baby forgets the five minutes of acute discomfort before the bottle is brought to him or her.

However, the point is not to explain the problem of suffering but rather to reassert our faith. The love of Mary for Jesus which we see in the Christmas crib scene is a reflection of God's love for us. Indeed, God's maternal concern for us is even greater than that which Mary had for Jesus. We honor Mary because she reflects God who has given birth to all of us and who renews our life constantly, promising us that eventually we will experience a life in which there will be only happiness and joy.

MARY AND JOSEPH

IT WAS very unlikely that Mary and Joseph would have given serious thought to ignoring the stipulations of the Law of Moses. It is safe to presume that they were deeply religious people and realized that the mere external observance of the Law was not enough to make a man pleasing to God. And yet, because keeping rules was not the fullness of the religious life, they did not thereby conclude that rules had nothing to do with the religious life. Rules may only be preliminary to authentic religion. They may do nothing more than create the order and the structure in which real religion can take place. Nevertheless, he who in the name of some romantic spiritual anarchy thinks he can dispense with order and rules does not really understand human nature. Salvation does not come from any law, whether one spells law with a capital L or a small l; but neither does it come from denying all laws, acting against laws, or by considering oneself superior to law. Mary and Joseph honored the Law of Moses because they realized that such honor was necessary to hold the Jewish people together. The law of any society may seem minor and unimportant, but mankind has learned that without a framework of law, human life and human religion become impossible. This is not to say that all law is perfect, that all law is just, or that the administration of law is always intelligent and sensitive to human needs. Law can fail; it must constantly be reformed (indeed Jesus came to replace the old Law with a very different kind of religious message). A law that is stagnant can become a law of tyranny and oppression; but a society without law can become a society in which anarchy turns into oppression. Law is not enough for man but man can't live without it. There may be too much law in the church today, and some of it may be a burden to the past and to the present, but it does not follow that the church can dispense with law.

The most obvious thing about the Magnificat is its combination

179

of confidence and humility. Mary is depicted both as rejoicing over the great triumphs of Yahweh and over her share in those triumphs. Also she is acknowledging her own role as the lowly suffering servant of Deutero-Isaiah. Even if we grant that this combination was to some extent part of the religious environment in which Mary and Jesus lived and on which Luke drew to write his gospel, we must still acknowledge that the fullness of the paradox was only achieved in Christianity; for it was only in Christianity, as Paul Ricoeur points out, that the eschatological Son of Man coming in power and majesty to judge the world is equated with the Suffering Servant, the most despised and abject of men. In other words, God, in the Christian belief, came to judge men precisely as a Suffering Servant who would die out of his love for them. The Magnificat, then, can be seen as a theme not only for Mary's life but for the life of her son, and, indeed, for the whole of Christian history—the theme of eschatological triumph through suffering and death.

Mary, in her proper place in Christian devotion, stands for the church. Just as she brought Jesus into the world initially, so the church brings him into the world today. Just as she was aware both of her eschatological and servant dimensions, so the church must, too, be aware of the fact that it is both a judge and a servant, though, like Mary and her son, it judges primarily by being a suffering servant. Just as Mary was content with a lowly role and did not try to stand between Jesus and his work, so the church must realize that it, too, is a handmaid of the Lord and must not permit itself to stand between the message of Jesus and the people for whom that message was intended. There is a good deal of room for triumph in the church, because sin and death have been conquered, and the church has participated in that conquest; but there is no room for triumphalism, both because the conquest was primarily the work of Jesus and not of his followers, and because there is no room at all in the image of the suffering servant for the slightest taint of triumphalism. Jesus was not a triumphalist, Mary was not a triumphalist. And when some members of the church become so enamored of their eschatological role that they forget the role of the suffering servant, they are not true to the Christian tradition or to the example that Mary has set for all of those "who belong to Him."

BE CONFIDENT

JESUS seemed to have a special attraction for pushy people. The Canaanite woman whose daughter was sick, Mary Magdalene pushing her way into the dinner to anoint his feet, the tax collector who climbed a tree to see him passing by, the Roman centurion who came to ask for his son's health, the blind beggar—all of these people received a quick and favorable response from Jesus. It was almost as though he saw in them something he felt in himself.

That Jesus found such people attractive should not be surprising. The principal thrust of his teaching was that we ought to be confident, that God's love for us was so powerful and so great that there was absolutely no reason to be timid or afraid. But most of the people who listened to Jesus then (as now) were narrow, suspicious, frightened, distrustful, cynical. Hence when Jesus encountered someone who could overcome such small and petty emotions and speak out bravely, forcefully and resolutely for what they wanted, he was impressed. Here was someone after his own heart, here was someone who believed that it was safe to take chances when dealing with God.

Diffidence and cowardice are not what God wants. Bartimaeus the blind beggar knew that he was completely dependent on Jesus for help; he pleaded with him for mercy. And yet there was something dignified and authentic about Bartimaeus' stance. He did not whine, he did not grovel; he shouted what he wanted at the top of his lungs—and he got it. One wonders what Jesus would have thought if Bartimaeus had sat by the side of the road and mumbled in a low voice, as we used to at the stations of the cross, "I am a worm, and no man."

If we are confident in our religious life, then many of the other fears and worries that plague us will seem less important. If we really believe that God's love is so powerful that it will protect us even from death, then there may not be very many other things that are worth worrying about. Jesus came to preach that there is, in the final analysis, nothing of which we should be afraid. The ultimate sin—and perhaps in a way the only sin—is the sin of not believing in the power of God's love. Whatever his frailties may have been, Bartimaeus was not deficient in confidence in God's love. And that was all he really needed.

Chapter Eight

The New Agenda

THE NEW AGENDA: 1972

A MERICAN Catholicism is going through a period of emotional exhaustion. Powerful currents of excitement, hope,
disappointment, anger, frustration, and bitterness have swept the
Church. Now our energies are spent. We are weary of controversy, of stridency, of the cycle of elation and discouragement which
has been typical of the last several years. We are no longer capable
of caring what the papacy or the national hierarchy or even our
own bishop says or does. We are weary of reading and of writing,
of bishops, of ex-priests, of new nuns, of revolutionaries, of noise,
of protest, of threat, of confrontation. We simply want to be left
alone. We do our work and live our lives; we stay away from
meetings and lectures; we skip news stories whose headlines begin
"pope warns" or "theologian attacks." We find ourselves wondering who cares what the pope has to say or what the theologians
have to say.

Everyone used to ask, "When will it all end?"—the right wing
wondering when the revolutionary turbulence would end and the
left wing wondering when the old style of ecclesiastical organization and administration would end. On both sides we now know
that the answer to the question is, "It's not going to end and we
are going to live in a time of chaos and confusion for the rest of
our lives." So we say to hell with it and try to forget the last decade
like it was a bad dream. We are in a time of pause, a despair of
numbness, of apathy, of indifference. As the sociologist, Peter
Berger, recently observed, the reason that all revolutions eventually come to an end is that even revolutionaries have to sleep.
There are not all that many revolutionaries in the American Church
but even the non-revolutionaries want, if not to sleep, at least to
enjoy a little bit of peace and quiet.

For we are tired; tired of enthusiasm, tired of the steady stream
of magic answers that came along each year, the cursillo, sensi-

187

tivity, kerygmatic catechetics, priests' organizations, lay organizations, nuns' organizations, pentecostals; all these were tried and failed. We are tired of the promise of such new movements and we are tired of the disappointment that comes upon us when we discover that while they have something to offer, they are really not the all-purpose answers that they purported to be.

And come to think of it, the thing we are most tired of is the "expert" with the answer. We wish all the experts would go away with all their answers and leave us alone. . . .

I propose to list eight areas with which I think the new agenda should deal and I will indicate very tentatively, more as a basis for discussion than anything else, the direction in which I think we are going to have to go in phrasing the questions.

1. *Faith.* The approach to faith in the old Church was apologetic. It was necessary that we have "answers" to all possible questions even if it was unlikely that anybody was going to ask us the questions. We could prove that there was a God, that Jesus was the Messiah, that he died and rose from the dead, that he founded the Church, that the pope was the head of the Church, that the pope was infallible, that birth control was wrong, and that one could never lose the faith without ever having first sinned. We were supposed to have all the appropriate "proofs" at our fingertips, if not to refute others, at least to reassure ourselves in times of trouble and doubt. It is easy to ridicule this intellectualist approach to religious faith but hindsight ridicule is always easy and always cheap. Apologetic faith was a response to a situation in which the Church found itself. The situation has changed and the response must change.

But most of the dialogue of the last five years is set within the context of the old question. We were once able to prove that there was a God. Now we are troubled by the thought that maybe we can't prove that there is a God, that in fact maybe God is dead. We used to be able to prove that the accounts of the Resurrection were not legends; now we are faced with the thought that most of the Resurrection stories are legendary (though the fact of the apostles' Easter experience is anything but legendary). We used to be able to prove that Jesus claimed he was the Messiah and now we know that it is extremely unlikely that Jesus used that title or indeed any title of himself. We used to have to insist vigorously that there was a personal God and now we find ourselves agonizing over the question of whether God is a person at all.

In other words, what used to be proven is now in doubt and the old proofs will not eliminate the new doubts but neither will the new doubts give us any religious direction to go in. If we are to get out of the dilemma, we must rephrase the question.

The question "Is there a God?" is one of the most foolish questions that men could ever ask. The pertinent question today, as at most other times in the course of human history, is rather "Who is *your* God?"; that is to say, what are your religious symbols and, particularly, what is your most "privileged" religious symbol. Tell us about the nature of the Real. What sort of answer does your symbol system provide to fundamental questions about the benignity of being, the purposefulness of human life, the worth and dignity of human existence. How do your symbols resolve the question about whether life is arbitrary and capricious or benign and gracious? . . .

2. *Community.* In the immigrant Church, the question was whether you belonged to the parish community or not. And you belonged to the parish community by going to Mass, receiving the sacraments, contributing to the support of the pastor, sending your children to parochial school, and belonging to parish societies. In the last half-decade, it has been argued that the traditional parish was outmoded and that one could be part of a community of Christians and not perform all, or even necessarily any, of the old community requirements. It used to be said that you couldn't be a good Catholic and not go to Mass on Sunday. Now the brave new rad-

icals proclaim that they can be good Catholics and not go to Mass on Sunday.

But on the new agenda the question of Sunday Mass attendance will not loom as being very important nor will the issue of old parish versus new "floating" parish be especially pertinent. What will be asked, rather, will be how Christians can come together to support one another in their family lives, their work lives, their political, social, and educational commitments. One does not become an active Christian merely by bravely proclaiming that it is no longer necessary to go to Mass on Sunday. But one thing is quite certain: nobody becomes an active Christian by himself. The critical question, then, whether in large parish or small community, becomes how do we band together with our brothers and sisters to provide the most effective religious support possible?

3. *Education.* There can be no doubt that the parochial school was at the center of the immigrant parish nor can there be any doubt that opposition to the parochial school was the hallmark of Catholic liberalism, so the whole question of Christian education was set in a context of support for or opposition to parochial schools. It was either the school or CCD, school or religious education; but such a statement of the question ignored the fact that relatively little is accomplished by formal education—be it in school or out of school—if the way is not prepared by the family environment (the most obvious finding of the Greeley-Rossi report and the one most frequently ignored by both sides of the controversy). From what we now know of the human developmental process, it should be clear that a young person absorbs his world-view in the very earliest years of life in about the same way he learns his language and his sexual identity—by imitating the behavior of his parents. The basic question, then, of Christian education is not whether people should go to parochial schools or not, but how the interreaction of parents with one another and their separate

and joint view of the world beyond the family is absorbed by the child in the earliest years of life and grows and develops as the child matures in the context of the family environment. Courses, curricula, textbooks, methods of religious instruction, be they in school or in less formal educational environments, are of minor moment compared to the context of the family relationship. The issue for the new agenda, then, is not should we have parochial schools (we probably will have them in some form) but rather what sort of attitudes and behavior on the part of parents can most effectively communicate Christian values to their children.

4. *Church Structure.* Church structures are currently in a state of collapse and the argument rages now among three groups: those who think all structures should be abandoned, those who think all structures should be preserved, and that dwindling group in the middle that believes in reforming Church structures.

But it is a foolish controversy. All human communities have some kind of established patterns of behavior. The fundamental issue is not whether priests marry, or whether priests become more effective with lay people if they wear sport clothes, tell dirty jokes, and insist that they be called by their first names; the basic question, rather, is how the Christian people and their religious leadership will relate to one another. Will the leadership be content with denouncing the people either on the one hand as bigots and racists or on the other, as pagan materialists; or will priests and people learn how to relate to one another as friends, people who can give and exchange support, encouragement, comfort and challenge. In the old days, the official leaders were thought to have a monopoly on leadership; in the last half-decade, many younger clergy and religious have tried to abandon their leadership role altogether. But the issue is not whether a priest can stop being a leader. If he stops being a leader the Christian community will find itself another priest, for all religious communities require leadership.

The question is, rather, how can leader and community most appropriately make demands on one another and how can they most effectively comfort and support one another.

5. *Ritual.* In the old Church we had the Byzantine ceremony of the Latin Mass as official devotion and rosary, daily communion, benediction, novenas, days of recollection, retreats, and so forth, as the quasi-official popular devotions. Both varieties of ritual have been abandoned for the new liturgy which at best is mildly impressive and at worst an awful bore. A priest who mumbles Mass in English facing the people turns out to be not much of an improvement over a priest who mumbled the Mass in Latin with his back to the people. A lay reader unintelligently stumbling through an Epistle he does not understand is not better than a priest stumbling through an Epistle he did not understand. Guitar music that most of the congregation cannot sing is in no way an improvement over organ music that most of the congregation cannot sing. And the principal benefit for most people of the English liturgy is now that it takes place in their own language they can realize how unsatisfactory as a community love feast the Mass in its present form really is.

But the question is not whether liturgy will be secular or sacred, whether it will be high church or low church, whether it will be sedate or swinging, whether the music will be polyphonic or hard rock. The real question is, rather, what kinds of ceremony, what sorts of prayers, public and private, will most effectively respond to the religious needs of modern urban man.

We were told not so long ago that action and discussion were for many people an adequate substitute for contemplation and that, in the modern world, solitude and reflection were irrelevant. Then the Zen Buddhists and the yoga devotees arrived on the scene and it turned out that solitude was not after all irrelevant and that not all prayer had to be accompanied by a strumming guitar or take place in a group of people holding hands with one another. The issue is not how far one can go in liturgical innovation (obviously at this point one can go as far as one wants to go; church leadership has completely lost control of liturgical innovation). The question is rather what are the religious needs that lurk in the depths of the soul of contemporary man and what sorts of ritual and liturgy will most effectively respond to those needs in the context of the Christian system of symbol and myth. It is an excellent question and I would submit that no one I know has even the beginnings of an answer to it.

6. *Mysticism versus relevance.* Closely related to the question of liturgy is the question of whether we ought to withdraw from the world or be involved in it. Are we monastic or secular? Are we contemplative or activist? Do we best witness the gospel by losing ourselves in mystical ecstasy or by being out on the picket lines? In the immigrant Church the mystical emphasis was dominant though, if the truth be told, it was a strange kind of mysticism which equated the contemplative life with internal organizational activity in the Church. For all the warning about the heresy of action, we heard very little about John of the Cross or Meister Eckhart. But in the last several years all the emphasis has been on "relevance." The Church has rather little to give the secular world we are told and much to learn from it. Contemplation, mysticism are copouts. Man no longer needs the sacred and if we are to make any progress at all we must become relevant to human social problems.

This is mostly nonsense. I must insist from a greater experience of the world beyond the Church than most American Catholic commentators have that it is the word of God that people are most eager to hear. I made the astonishing discovery in my course this autumn that almost all of my students were deeply concerned about the "crisis of the middle years." Even though they were all in their twenties, and most of them are in their early twenties, they had seen what the crisis of the middle years meant to their parents, and were terribly afraid of decisions which would make it impossible for them in their own time to cope with a similar crisis. A number of them pointed out to me they were afraid to get married, to have children, to choose a career because such commitments might close off all their options and trap them in a set of circumstances which would wreck their lives before they were forty-five. They admitted this fear of the middle years was a crisis of nerve and a manifestation of extraordinary conservatism but, as one girl pointed out to me, "How can I possibly commit myself to all the repsonsibilities of really being an adult unless I have something to believe in, something that will sustain me through all the problems and crises of raising my own children?"

So the question isn't mysticism versus involvement, or the Church teaching the world versus the Church learning from the world. The question is, rather, how we combine mysticism and involvement, how we simultaneously preach the Good News and listen to human longings for the Good News. To put the matter even more bluntly, the old question was, "How ought Catholics to be different from others?" The new response during the last several years is to say that Catholics are no different from anyone else, but on the emerging agenda, the question has to be rephrased: "What unique contributions can Catholics make to the human longing for purpose and involvement?"

7. *Sexuality.* In the old Church, we took our stand against abortion, birth control, working wives, and in favor of Cana, CFM, and large families. In the dialogue of the last four or five years, the radical position has been in favor of birth control, against large families (perhaps in favor of abortion or at least ambivalent about it), and in favor of women's liberation. The real problem with women's liberation is that it does not go far enough. It does not address itself to the profound changes in human attitudes and behavior that are required if men and women are to relate to one another as friends and equals, and if men are to be free to develop

194

tenderness and women free to develop professional commitments. On the old agenda, we argued about premarital and extramarital sex, and perhaps more recently about homosexuality. On the new agenda, we will ask, perhaps using Paul Tillich's method of correlation, what light the Christian symbol system sheds on the ambiguity of human sexuality, and we will discover that the answer is that since God loves us it is all right to trust ourselves to be vulnerable in loving relationships with others.

8. *Asceticism.* In the church before the council the perfection of the Christian life was thought to consist in self-denial and sacrifice. The more you "gave up" the better you were and the best people gave up practically everything. Poverty, chastity and obedience were virtuous because they were means by which one could deprive oneself of possessions, pleasure and power. Life was a constant struggle to keep unruly impulses and passions under control. The new answer to the old question, "what do we have to give up?" is: "practically nothing." We are supposed to "enjoy," to "celebrate," to "do our own thing," to give ourselves over to self-fulfillment. But the self-fulfillment ethic, particularly in the shallow version in which it is preached by some clergy and religious is a truncated version of existentialism and personalism which Freud, Camus, and Kierkegaard, each for more or less the same reason, would dismiss as infantile or adolescent behavior. Authentic personalism demands strength, courage, discipline, responsibility. One cannot be "concerned for the other" unless one has extraordinary control over one's energies and resources and the ability to focus and direct one's talents and behavior. Self-fulfillment does not mean following one's instincts but rather asserting the control of one's highest and most noble aspirations over one's fears and suspicions. The pertinent question is not, "what do we have to give up" but, "how does our Christian faith enable us to become mature, responsible adults who can focus our instincts instead of being ruled by them." The answer, I suspect,

is to be found in a deeper understanding of the cross and resurrection symbol. . . . Jesus could only rise after he died. The cross was a necessary prelude to the new life. Growth in maturity requires death to selfishness, irresponsibility, undisciplined instinct so that we may rise to a new life of mature, generous, trusting freedom. The cross and resurrection symbols help us to die the death required for maturity because they assure us that our struggles for life are not in vain.

I will concede that there is an imprecision in the phrasing of the new questions but if I could phrase them precisely the new agenda would have already emerged instead of having just begun to appear. We must ask what our religious symbols mean, how it is possible for us to provide religious support for one another; how we pass on religious values to our children; how priests and people can relate to each other in love, encouragement, challenge and affection; what sort of worship is most appropriate to our needs; how men and women can learn to live with one another in trust, respect, affection, and equality. How do we combine contemplation and involvement, mysticism and relevance, preaching the gospel and reading the signs of our times?

To address ourselves to these questions means not merely to give up the answers of the immigrant Church but also to give up the allegedly new responses which are still imprisoned within the perspectives of immigrant Catholicism. It will be very difficult to make the sacrifice. It will mean that we will have to stop arguing about the existence of God, about parochial schools, about Church structures, about birth control and abortion, about married priests and religious garb, and about how Catholics are different from others. These are peripheral questions compared with the items I am suggesting should be on the new agenda. They may not be totally unimportant but they cannot be answered effectively unless we leave them aside so that we can address ourselves to more fundamental issues.

The trouble is that we are only beginning now to know how to phrase those fundamental issues and it will take many years before the issues are clearly and precisely stated.

Many times when one speaks to Catholic groups about these new questions, particularly priests and nuns, one encounters a hostile reaction. It is said in the audience that, after all, the people who are here are simple, hard working priests or teachers. They have problems to deal with in their parishes or their schools. They have come to the lectures to learn how to respond to those problems. They see no point in coming to a lecture just to hear more complicated questions.

The response is understandable but I think it betrays one of the fundamental weaknesses of contemporary American Catholicism: our passion for the practical program as a substitute for the elaboration of new theory. We have gone about as far as we can go on sheer pragmatic programming. Whether we like it or not, we now must address ourselves to questions for which there are no answers and for which there will not be answers for a long time to come. However great the practical problems may be in our parishes and our schools, however necessary it is to respond as best we can to those problems, we have to face the fact that the really critical need in the Church is the elaboration of new theory. We had a theory once; it collapsed during the 1960s. Most of the discussion that went on in the Church in the late 1960s and led to our present emotional exhaustion was still defined in the terms and the categories of the old theory. We are now in a state of weariness and collapse because, for all our enthusiasm and energy, we could not build a new Church on the mirror of the old theory.

We will need scholarship, thought, experimentation, poetry, prophesy, and sanctity to evolve the new agenda, to begin to formulate answers to the questions that that agenda will eventually specify. It is time that we begin.

THE NEW AGENDA—1985

I HAVE four modest suggestions—and it is an indication of the nature of the turmoil in the church today and of the collapse of conversation between the upper church and the lower church (the subject of one of my recommendations) that the American hierarchy cannot, without causing enormous trouble for itself with Rome, discuss these recommendations, cannot even admit they have been made.

1. The leadership of the church ought to strive to establish institutions of upward communication by which it can listen more closely and more sensitively to the laity's experience of God and life. Theologically this might be called consulting the faithful, or discerning the spirit, or ascertaining the "consensus fidelium." Pope John Paul in his exhortation *Familiaris consortio* has said, as I noted before, explicitly that the laity have a unique and indispensable contribution to make to the church's self-awareness in matters related to marriage. One would argue, however, only with blindness to the facts that the laity have been given an opportunity to make their unique and indispensable contribution. It is important to understand today that American Catholics are not saying that birth control and premarital sex are sinful but they're going to do it anyway—they are, rather, saying that it is not sinful to divorce sex from procreation and even sex from permanent commitment. Apparently they have most of their clergy on their side in the first assertion and many of their clergy on their side in the second assertion. Thus far the hierarchy and the papacy have responded by saying in effect, "You're wrong, that's all. There's nothing to discuss because you're wrong!"

(Personally, I think I can understand what they're saying when they say that the experience of marriage persuades them that sex can be divorced from procreation. I also think that most of the data from the human sciences, comparative primatology, teleo-anthropology, etc., lends some support for this position. I will admit, however, that I really don't understand their apparent insistence that sex can be divorced from permanent and public commitment. I do not believe that premarital sex is the greatest evil in the world by any means but I am astonished that so many of the laity so quickly have come to the conclusion that it isn't really very evil at all.)

I am not suggesting that the institutional church simply cave in to this insistence of the laity that it misunderstands the human experience of sex, I am merely recommending, as Archbishop John R. Quinn did in his address at the synod of the family in 1980 that there be dialogue between the laity and the hierarchy on this subject in which the hierarchy listen carefully and try to discern perhaps more sensitively than it has hitherto what the Holy Spirit might be saying to the church through, to quote John Paul again, "the unique and indispensable contribution" of the married laity.

Will such dialogue happen? Of course not—and hence the non-dialogue and the turbulence and the crises will continue.

2. It would be helpful if scholars and leaders, theologians and teachers, artists and writers, bent their efforts to development of a positive, constructive approach to human sexuality in which the church was seen as clearly supporting the attempts of the married lay people to grow in love of one another and of God through their marital intimacy. To sustain sexual passion (which is a sacrament of God's passionate love for us) through the long years of a marriage requires patience, sensitivity, discipline, tenderness, courage, vulnerability and the perennial willingness to start anew, to begin again, to be reborn. There is no reason to think that men and women living in the post-Freudian era have any more skills at these difficult virtues than did their predecessors. But surely the church has something to say about the motivations required to develop such skills. John Paul II's audience talks on human sexuality having

set the context and provided the raw material and philosophical and theological reflection, now would certainly be the proper time for the church to encourage, support, facilitate and even push the development of such a positive and constructive theory of sexuality. No less a person than Cardinal Bernardin suggested that at the synod on the family—and seems to have been ignored by everyone.

There is so much anger, resentment, bitterness, sullen and stubborn animosity, that no one, neither the hierarchy nor the theologians nor the clergy nor, with few exceptions, writers, artists and story tellers, are going even to attempt such a positive theory of sexuality until they sniff some winds of change from Rome, winds for which they surely will sniff in vain for the imaginable future. This refusal to do what is well within the capacity of the heritage to begin to do seems to me to be comparable to the loss of nerve among the clergy and the loss of confidence among Catholic educators. Even though Catholic schools are more important than they ever were and priests are more important than they ever were, both the educators and the clergy refuse to abandon their crisis of identity. And, even though the time is especially appropriate to develop a positive and constructive Catholic theory of sexuality, those who might be able to do so adamantly and stubbornly refuse to begin. Their attitude often seems to be that they'll "be damned if we'll do it, until the church changes on birth control." It seems to me to be a foolish position but it is one that is not going to be changed. Better to cheer for the Sandanistas and for other Marxist/Leninist regimes around the world, than to work on a positive Catholic theory of sex.

3. Since the religious imagination is so important and since the Catholic religious sensibility has changed so notably in the last twenty years, it would make sense, would it not, for the institutional church to begin to take more seriously those works which have impact primarily on the imagination—art, music, literature,

sculpture, architecture. Knowing that there is not the chance of
an ice cube in purgatory that anyone will take this recommendation seriously, I would nonetheless recommend in the time of an
emerging new religious sensibility that the church renew its traditional commitment to the arts, fine and lively, that was once so
much taken for granted that no one would have dreamed it possible the church would have abandoned the arts as it has. The artist
(musician, story teller, poet) is a "sacrament maker," a person
who calls out of his materials insights and images into the meaning that lurks beneath them. For most of its history the Catholic
Church has realized that the sacrament makers are not luxuries
but necessities for its life and work. One would like to think that
as a new religious sensibility develops the church leadership will
understand that the only way it can guide and direct the development of that religious sensibility is not denouncing it, not trying
to limit it or contain it, but rather influencing its direction and
flow through works of the fine and lively arts.

4. Since the quality of Sunday preaching is such an important
influence in the life of the lay people and since they rate that quality
so low, it might be wise to attempt to improve the quality of
preaching. The synod after the Extraordinary Synod is to be
devoted to the laity. The laity themselves will not of course participate, save perhaps through carefully chosen and untypical
tokenism; if the American Catholic laity were permitted to participate and the subject of Sunday preaching was raised, they would
probably talk of no other subject until the bishops went home.

I know from previous experience that I might as well cut paper
dolls out of the pages of this book as to recommend that something
be done about the poor homilies the laity must sit through every
weekend. The bishops and the clergy are now greatly exercised
about the rights of the poor, but singularly disinterested in the right
of the laity to have the gospel effectively preached to them, a right
in strict commutative justice with an obligation to restitution.

Other people are bound to justice, it would seem, not Sunday homilists.

Better sermons, more concern about works of the imagination, a positive theory of sexual intimacy, more careful attention to the actual experience of the laity—surely not an unreasonable agenda of policy issues.

SOURCE IDENTIFICATION

With the exception of two excerpts from *The Critic* magazine all books cited are published by The Thomas More Press, 223 West Erie St., Chicago, IL 60610.

Chapter One

A Tale of Two Parishes — *What a Modern Catholic Believes about the Church*

Don't Just Give Me Orders — *Parish, Priest & People*

Did Jesus Really Establish the Church? — *Bottom Line Catechism*

The Hierarchy as Scapegoat — *Everything You Wanted to Know about the Church...*

Why Has Ecumenism Failed? — *The Catholic Why? Book*

The "Neighborhood" Church vs. the "Downtown" Church — *Crisis in the Church*

Chapter Two

Today's Priest: Unsure and Arrogant — *Tomorrow's Church*

Why Is the Priesthood a Permanent State? — *The Catholic Why? Book*

Why Have So Many Priests and Nuns Abandoned Their Vocations? — *The Catholic Why? Book*

The Vocation Problem — *American Catholics Since the Council*

Married Priests? — *Everything You Wanted to Know about the Church...*

Recommendations to Present and Future Priests — *Parish, Priest & People*

An Andrew Greeley Reader